D1564895

PERSONAL SOUL - WINNING

PERSONAL SOUL-WINNING

By WILLIAM EVANS, Ph. D., D. D., Litt. D.

Bible Teacher and Director of Bible Conferences
Author of "The Book of Books," "How to
Memorize," "Outline Study of the Bible,"
"How to Prepare Sermons and Gospel
Addresses," "The Book-Method
of Bible Study," etc.

MOODY PRESS • CHICAGO

Printed in United States of America

FOREWORD.

No higher honor could be conferred upon the Christian, and no greater privilege be given the believer in Jesus Christ than to be associated with Him in the great and blessed work of bringing a lost world to the knowledge of the truth. This is Christlike: "For the Son of man is come to seek and to save that which was lost" (Luke 19:10).

It is not possible for every Christian to be a preacher or a teacher in spiritual things, for these are special gifts bestowed by the Holy Spirit upon certain believers, even as it hath pleased Him. But there is no Christian, however humble or insignificant he may feel himself, or others esteem him to be, who is not appointed by the Spirit to be a winner of souls. One often wonders whether the honor conferred upon the believer of being a soul-winner is not greater than the conferred gift of teaching or preaching; and whether or not at the last day, when the rewards are distributed, the personal soul-winner will receive as great, if not a greater reward than many a teacher or preacher. Daniel 12:3 (R. V.) is filled with glorious comfort for the man who seeks to turn sinners to God: "And they that be teachers shall shine as the brightness of the firmament; and they that turn many to righteousness, as the stars forever and ever."

That the individual Christian may be prompted, encouraged, and equipped to do this kind of Personal Soul-Winning work, is the purpose of this book. Its popular or conversational style of address will, it is hoped, enable the book to more thoroughly accomplish its purpose. The leading Scripture references have

been made to stand out distinctly from the main body
of type in order that they may be easily located.

WILLIAM EVANS.

CONTENTS.

THE VALUE OF PERSONAL
EFFORT IN SOUL-WINNING

CHAPTER I.

THE VALUE OF PERSONAL EFFORT IN SOUL WINNING.

EVERY Christian should consider it the highest honor, and the greatest privilege to assist in the growth of the kingdom of God, by personal effort in individual soul-winning. He should realize, too, that it is not only his privilege to thus work for God, but that a most solemn responsibility rests upon him to do so. The true Christian, having found Christ to be precious to his own soul, desires, or at once seeks, as did Andrew and Philip of old, to get someone else to taste and see that the Lord is good.

And what is true of the individual Christian should be true of the whole Church. What is the true position of the Church according to the teachings of Christ? Is she not to be the salt of the earth and the light of the world? Should she not be as the woman seeking the lost coin, the shepherd seeking the straying sheep, and the father on the constant lookout for the wayward son? That church, the members of which are not interested in, and putting forth personal effort in behalf of, a lost world, has in truth forfeited its credentials and its right to exist. In seeking to save its own soul, it has really lost it

An anonymous clipping contains the following suggestive remarks along this particular line:

"'What man of you, having an hundred sheep, if he lose one of them, doth not leave the ninety and nine in the wilderness, and go after that which is lost, until he find it?' That is to say, the alpha and omega of

Christianity is soul-winning, and every letter between the first and last should be permeated by the spirit which seeks the lost.

"It is not enough to be evangelical. We must be evangelistic. The evangelical church is a reservoir of pure water without a pipe running anywhere. If you will take the trouble to go to it and climb the embankment, you will get a good drink. The evangelistic church is a reservoir of pure water with a pipe to every heart in the community, and every nation in the world. Evangelical may mean truth on ice; evangelistic means truth on fire. Evangelical may be bomb-proof for defense; evangelistic means an army on the march with every face towards the enemy. Evangelical sings, 'Hold the fort, for I am coming'; evangelistic sings, 'Storm the fort, for God is leading.' The need of the Church is not evangelicalism as a thing to fight for, but evangelism as a force to fight with. The evangelical creed merely held and defended becomes a fossil, only a thing of interest.

"Several miles above Milton, Pa., when the ice was breaking up, a farmer got into one of his boats, purposing to pull it out of the river. A floating mass of ice struck it, breaking it loose from the bank, and carrying it and him out into the current. A neighbor, seeing the danger, mounted a horse and with all speed rode down to Milton. The people of the town gathered all the ropes they could secure, went out on the bridge, and suspended a line of dangling ropes from the bridge across the river. They could not tell at just what point the boat with the farmer would pass under, so they put a rope down every two or three feet clear across. By and by the farmer was seen, wet and cold, standing in the boat half full of water, drifting down the rapid current. When he saw the ropes dangling within reach. he seized the nearest one, was drawn up and saved. Now, one rope might not have answered the purpose. The pastor hangs the rope of salvation from the pulpit, and sinners present do not seem to get near it; but if the business men will hang out ropes, and you young men and women, mothers and wives, hang out ropes, sinners will certainly be saved."

Greater stress is here laid upon winning men to Christ by individual effort rather than upon any other method of accomplishing the same purpose, revivals, for example. Not that we do not believe in revivals, for how can one be a believer in the Bible and not believe in revivals? But personal soul-winning is much greater than revivalism. Indeed, is not the purpose and end of a true revival to make the individual Christian worker more interested in souls? A revival that does not accomplish this end is not a success. Both evangelist and pastor agree on this.

Revivalism is fishing with a great net; personal soul-winning is fishing with a single hook. Both are right; but all Christians cannot handle the big net, while all can use the single hook. All Christians are to be fishers of men. That form of Christian activity, therefore, is most important, which excludes none from participation in it.

Much is said today about winning "the crowds" for Jesus Christ. Every such effort is to be encouraged; but we must not forget that men can enter into the kingdom of God only as individuals. Religion emphasizes personality. In what is a man better than a sheep? In this: that he is a personality, and must be dealt with as such, personally, individually. It is for this reason that the intelligent evangelist lays such emphasis upon a good corps of personal workers who shall deal with the people that come forward under the impulse of the invitation, individually and personally. Indeed, we do not consider that converts have been dealt with properly until they have been dealt with personally.

Religion emphasizes personality. Recently a photograph was left in my office. It was that of a converted convict. It had no name on it, only a number. Personality is lost in jail; it is a number that is there recognized. It is a number that paces up and down the cell, a number that walks out to work in the yards, a number that sits down to eat, a number that takes sick and dies, and a number that is buried in the potter's field. Personality, not numbers, counts in the kingdom of God; the Church is made up of that innumerable host which no man can number, but who carry upon their foreheads the name of Him whose they are and whom they serve. All talk about a social salvation, and a sweeping of men into the kingdom by crowds, is to be received with some apprehension, to say the least.

JESUS CHRIST OUR EXAMPLE.

Jesus Christ won most, if not all, of His followers by personal effort. Do you recall a single instance of what we, in this day, would call a great revival taking place during Christ's ministry? He enlisted Matthew at the toll-booth, and Peter, James and John at their nets, by personal invitation: "Come, follow me!" One by one, man by man; that is how Christ's cause grew.

What is the great lesson taught in the first chapter of John, the chapter commonly called the "Eureka" or "I have found" chapter? Is it not that the Church of Christ grew and is to grow by personal effort? Does not the Holy Spirit set forth at the beginning of the Christian dispensation the divine method of extending Christianity, the law of the kingdom's growth, namely, the finding of one disciple by another?

The supreme business of the Christian is to individualize the Gospel. No distinction, such as clergy and laity, is here recognized. As followers of Christ we are all to be personal soul-winners. Every Christian layman is "ordained" to go and bring forth fruit, and is a "minister" in so far as every man who has received a gift—and every Christian has received one—is called upon to minister therewith (John 15:16; 1 Peter 4:10, 11).

THE APOSTLES' EXAMPLE.

How personal soul-winning is emphasized in the Acts of the Apostles! Pentecost is passed over with comparatively small mention; but the Church of Jesus Christ going out as individual personal workers—John here, Peter there, Philip yonder, the ordinary Christian layman going from house to house, seeking to extend the kingdom of the Christ—this is given in detail, and to its narration is devoted much space.

THE TESTIMONY OF TWO PASTORS.

The church at Colosse began not with a great revival under Paul, but as the result of the faithful personal work of one man, Epaphras. The church at Rome was undoubtedly founded in the same way. Pastors acknowledge that the best additions to their churches are those won to Christ by personal effort. Dr. Hughes, recently chosen bishop in the Methodist Episcopal Church, says, that in a revival in his church covering two years, there were 48 converts, 11 men and 37 women; but that, as a result of personal work during the same period, there were 75 converts, 40 men and 35 women. Is there not a lesson for us to learn from this experience, not only as to numbers, but as to sex? Here is the solution of the pastor's problem, "How to reach the men." Dr. J. O. Peck is reported to have said, that if he had the certainty that he was to live only ten years, and as a condition of gaining heaven at the end thereof, he had to win a thousand or ten thousand souls for Christ, and he was given his choice of winning them either by preaching sermons or by individual effort, he would choose the latter method every time.

ELEMENTS OF SUCCESS IN
PERSONAL SOUL-WINNING

CHAPTER II.

ELEMENTS OF SUCCESS IN PERSONAL SOUL-WINNING.

A MONG the elements of success in personal work may be mentioned:

1. Tact. Isaiah 50:4.

"Tact," according to the dictionary, "is a quick or intuitive appreciation of what is proper, fitting or right; the mental ability of doing and saying the right thing at the right time so as not to unjustly offend or anger."

In other words, tact is nothing more or less than skill and facility in dealing with men. Tact has been called the life of the five senses: it is the open eye, the quick ear, the judging taste, the keen smell, the lively touch. Tact knows what to do and when and how to do it.

Christ manifested great tact in His reply to the unreasonable question of the Pharisees, when He called for a coin, and in reply to the captious question of His enemies, said: "Render to Cæsar the things which are Cæsar's; and to God the things which are God's."

Paul showed tact when, brought before the tribunal, perceiving that his audience was divided on the question of the resurrection of the dead—the Pharisees believing it, and the Sadducees disbelieving it—he cried out: "For the hope of the resurrection of the dead am I called in question." His tact won the day; for we read, that, immediately following this appeal, there "arose a dissension between the Pharisees and the Sadducees: and the multitude was divided." In writing

to the Corinthians, Paul says: "Being crafty, I
caught you with guile."

A Salvation Army lass was once accosted by a young
dude whom she asked to buy a *War Cry* for five cents.
"Give me ten cents' worth of prayer," said the foolish
youth.   Instantly the lassie knelt down before the
young man and the young ladies who were accompany-
ing him, and prayed for the fellow.   And so earnestly
did the lassie pray that that young man sought her a
few days later and asked her to point him to a Saviour
who could save him from his waywardness and sin.
That young lassie had tact.

Philip the evangelist had tact, and manifested it in
dealing with the Ethiopian eunuch (Acts 8).   Instead
of blurting out, as many Christian workers do today:
"Are you a Christian? if not, you are going to hell;
repent, or you will be damned," he approached him
with the question, quite natural to a man who was
engaged in reading, "Understandest thou what thou
readest?" The result of such tactful dealing was that
the eunuch invited the evangelist to ride with him and
explain to him the way of salvation.   Ultimately the
man found Jesus Christ as his Saviour, and went on
his way rejoicing.   Many an untactful man would have
spoiled that magnificent opportunity.

Fishermen teach us the value of tact in their choice
and use of various kinds of bait, and in the different
methods pursued in catching different kinds of fish.

Tact supplies the lack of many talents; indeed, the
lack of it is oftentimes fatal.   A little tact and wise
management very often gain a point which could be
gained in no other way.

It is fortunate for the Christian worker that this
element of success in personal work is at his command.
It comes from God in answer to prayer.   If a man
does not have it by nature, he may have it by grace.

God will give it in answer to prayer. "If any of you lack wisdom [tact], let him ask of God, that giveth to all men [and women alike] liberally, and upbraideth not; and it shall be given him" (Jas. 1:5). Compare 1 John 2:29; Acts 13:9, 10.

2. Contact. Matthew 5:13.

Contact is defined as the coming together of two bodies in space. It means, in personal work, the coming into touch with your man. Contact is button-holing, "tackling" your man. A man may have all the tact in the world, but it will be useless unless he gets into contact with men. Contact is tact put into practice.

Samson had strength sufficient to pull down the great temple of the Philistines; but it was of no avail until he was put into contact with, and his arms enclosed, the mighty pillars which supported the massive temple. Of what use is all our knowledge of methods, if we do not go after men and deal with them individually?

Of what use is the sword if there is no battle to be fought, no cause to be defended, no victory to be won? You may have the finest fishing tackle that money can buy in the cupboard in your home, but it will not catch fish for you until you bring it into contact with the fish in the water. So a Christian worker may have fine tackle for spiritual fishing—a knowledge of the habits of men and a good knowledge of the various Scripture passages to use in catching them—and yet be utterly futile and useless as a personal worker unless he comes into contact with men.

There are two things to remember about contact: first, we must have contact with God; second, we must have contact with men. We must be heart-foremost with God if we would be head-foremost with men. Jacob is a good illustration of this. First, he wrestled with God, and then, as a result, he had power with men. Witness his victory over his brother Esau.

3. Ability.

Ability is defined as the power of bringing things to pass. Ability was characteristic of the life of Jesus. Again and again do we find the words, "And it came to pass."

(a) We need ability to read and understand men.

Jesus knew men. We are told in John 2:24, 25, that "Jesus knew all men . . . he knew what was in man." Just as the successful fisherman must understand the habits of fish, so must the successful personal worker understand the ways, reasonings, disputings, and methods of men. Different temperaments need to be dealt with in different ways. Study men as well as books.

(b) We need ability in the handling of the Bible.

We should be able to handle our Bibles and turn to the desired location as expertly as the book agent turns to his prospectus and the life insurance man to his book of tables.

Philip the evangelist would have lost a magnificent opportunity if he had not been able to find the place in the Scriptures where it is written. We must be experts in the handling of the Word of God. Sometimes to hesitate means to lose the case you are dealing with. See how quickly Jesus turned to just the place he wanted when he was called upon to read in the synagogue at Nazareth (Luke 4:17): "And when he had opened the book, he found the place where it was written." Ability to find the place where it is written inspires confidence in the inquirer, whereas hesitancy is a barrier to effective dealing. We need ability in handling the Bible, for three reasons:

First: To show men from the Word of God that they are sinners.

It need hardly be said that all men do not concede that they are sinners. In order to convince them of this fact, we need words that are divine. No words of ours can produce conviction of sin: God's Word alone can do that. It is the "sword of the Spirit" alone that can prevail in such a conflict as this, and the sword of the Spirit is the Word of God (Eph. 6:17).

Secondly: To point men who are convicted of sin to Jesus Christ, who is the Sin-bearer.

This can only be done by directing the thought of the inquirer to those passages of Scripture which set forth the death of Christ as the propitiation for the sins of men. No words of ours can give peace and assurance to souls that are burdened with the knowledge and guilt of sin. God must speak if men are to hear the words, "Go in peace; thy sins are forgiven thee."

Thirdly: We must use the Bible in order to establish men in the faith, and to direct them to the means of growth in the Christian life.

It is not enough that we get men saved. We must show them how to make a success of the Christian life; we must show them how to "grow in grace, and in the knowledge of our Lord and Saviour Jesus Christ" (2 Peter 3:18).

(c) Again, we need ability to bring about decisions.
Many Christian workers find themselves unable to bring the inquirer beyond a certain point. They can bring the inquirer to acknowledge his sinfulness and express his desire to accept Christ as his Saviour, but cannot get him to really DO IT; and so the earnest, anxious inquirer goes away unsaved, simply because the personal worker did not have the ability to bring things to a final issue. Anyone who has had any experience whatever in fishing knows that there is a

world of difference in having a fish nibble at your hook and in catching it, and landing it right in the boat. To have a fish nibble at your hook is a good thing; to be able to lift it out of the water is a better thing; to land it right in the boat is the best thing of it all. So it is in spiritual fishing—in the catching of men. It is good to find an inquirer; it is better to be able to show him the way of life; it is best to be able to get him to definitely accept Christ as his personal Saviour.

Ability, as all the other essential factors of successful soul-winning, is something within the reach of the humblest child of God. It, too, is a gift from God, and comes in answer to prayer. We are told in 1 Peter 4:11 that there is such a thing as "the ability which God giveth." Then let us ask God in prayer to grant us this power so that we shall be able to bring things to pass for Him.

4. The appreciation of opportunities.   (Eph. 5:16.)

An opportunity is defined as a time with favoring or propitious circumstances; a favorable chance.

The personal worker must be an opportunist; he must believe in opportunism. The buying up of opportunities for Christ is not to be understood as an effort to save hours which we might be tempted to waste from idleness, but the effort to so control our time that we shall not allow any selfish motive, any cowardly timidity, to stand in the way of our doing good. The Christian worker must emulate the merchant who is quick to seize every bargain that is passing before him. As he buys up goods, so we must buy up opportunities for doing good, and especially those opportunities which are afforded us of speaking to men about their souls.

Paul tells us to redeem the time. By that he seems to indicate that every moment has its opportunity as·

signed to it in the way of doing good. By doing duty at the moment of opportunity we make a purchase of it, and thus not only make gain for good and for Christ's kingdom, but also take away that time from the evil one, and thus reduce the power of his dominion. When we let an opportunity to speak to a soul go by we let Satan take the time from us, and thus we contract a debt. Much is said in market circles of "getting a corner on the market." Let us get a corner on time and buy up every opportunity for Christ.

Two or three things may be said in this connection:

(a) Do not force opportunities.

Force is the opposite of opportunity. If you are in constant and continual communion with God, He will direct you in this matter. The question may be asked, "Must we not then speak to people unless we are moved to do so?" Possibly the best answer to this question is, that if you are in continual fellowship with God, you will be moved whenever the opportunity is presented to you.

(b) Then again, *We should see to it that we miss no opportunities.*

As men in the gold fields are constantly on the lookout for gold veins, so should the personal worker be on the lookout for souls. Wherever we are, whatever we may be doing, wherever we may be going, we should be on the lookout for opportunities for personal dealing. Much, oh, how much depends upon the wise use of the opportune moment! "There is a season when it is good to take occasion by the hand."

(c) Finally, *The wise use of opportunities implies good planning of time.*

Many of us waste much time because we have no definite plan for that time. Again, many opportunities are lost because we do not give the proper relative value to time. Put first things first, the essential before the non-essential, the primary before the secondary.

Two reasons are given in the Scriptures for the wise use of time and opportunities: First, because the days are few, because the daytime is working time, and the night cometh—oh, how soon it cometh—when no man can work. We must work while it is day (Gal. 6:10). Second, because "the days are evil": that is to say, the times and circumstances of life do not lend themselves to such spiritual use of time. The world seems to be wholly occupied with the enjoyment of sin and selfish pleasure. Such a world is not a great encouragement to definite soul-winning work for God.

5. An absolute conviction of truth.

What is truth? The truth as it is in Christ Jesus— the truth as Jesus taught it, and as it is expressed in the Bible. The truth regarding man, his lost condition, and his salvability; the truth regarding the redemptive work of Jesus Christ and the possibilities of fallen man because of it; the truth regarding the future: that whosoever believeth shall be saved, and whosoever believeth not shall be condemned.

Doubt and indecision in the worker beget doubt and indecision in the inquirer. If you are not sure that men are lost, then there is not much use in your trying to save them. If there is no wreck, there is no use in putting out the lifeboat. If there is no one drowning, what is the use of throwing out the lifeline? If your neighbor's house is not on fire, what is the use of going to his house in the dark of the night, and arousing him and his family, and warning him of the danger? But if there is a shipwreck, if there is a man overboard, if your neighbor's house is on fire, then quickly and earnestly man the lifeboat, throw out the lifeline, give your neighbor warning. The personal worker must be fully assured of some things; and these are some of the things: that all men are sinners, and as such will be lost, unless Jesus save them; that Jesus died to save them, and by faith in Him, and that alone, they can be saved; that outside of the redemption that is in Christ Jesus all men are lost; that in Him men are saved. These are some of the truths concerning which the personal worker must not be in doubt if he is to be successful in winning men for Christ.

6. A faith that never despairs.

We must be able to see the germ of the saint in the chief of sinners, the fairest flower in Christ's garden in the outcast woman of the street. We must believe, as the genealogies of Jesus teach us, that Jesus came through all sorts of people in order that He might save all sorts of people. We must see all men, not as they are in themselves, but as they may be in the light of the cross of Christ. This is what Paul meant when he said he was determined to know no man after the flesh * * * If any man was in Christ Jesus, he was (or became) a new creature. (2 Cor. 5:17.) We are told that a very beautiful face of the Christ was once painted on a very soiled linen handkerchief. So can the image of Christ be painted upon the worst of men. Such men as John B. Gough and John G. Woolley, the gutter drunkards, and Jerry McAuley, the river pirate, may, yea, have become the great temperance orators, the successful mission workers. We must believe in a gospel of hope—not too quick to believe that there is such a thing as being past redemption point in the matter of salvation. "Is anything too hard for the Lord?" (Gen. 18:14)—this must be the watchword of the successful personal worker. We are to "despair of no man" (Luke 6:35, R. V., margin).

7. Infinite patience.

The personal worker must be able to endure the "contradiction of sinners against themselves," the senseless arguments of those who oppose themselves, the treachery and deceit of those who follow Christ for "the loaves and fishes." He will deal patiently with men who are weak and who backslide easily. He will be called upon to lift them up after they have fallen more than once or twice. Judson, in Burmah, unable to tell of conversions in his first report, said: "Permit us to labor in obscurity for twenty years, and you shall hear from us again." And he was heard from.

8. A deep sense of responsibility.

Every personal worker ought to read often the third and thirty-third chapters of Ezekiel. Possibly no part of the whole Bible sets forth the responsibility of one man for another as do these chapters. It may not be our responsibility to bring every individual to Christ; but it is our responsibility to see that Christ is brought to every individual. Every man may not want Christ; but Christ wants every man, and it is our business to let every man know that Christ wants him. God has appointed me "my brother's keeper," whether I will it or not. "When I say unto the wicked, O wicked man, thou shalt surely die; if thou dost not speak to warn the wicked from his way, that wicked man shall die in his iniquity: but his blood will I require at thine hand. Nevertheless, if thou warn the wicked of his way to turn from it: if he do not turn from his way, he shall die in his iniquity, but thou hast delivered thy soul" (Ezek. 33:8, 9).

Daniel Webster was once asked what was the most solemn thought he had ever entertained. In reply, he said: "My personal responsibility to God." Can there be any more solemn thought than this for a Christian worker?

THE PERSONAL WORKER HIM-
SELF—HIS QUALIFICATIONS

CHAPTER III.

THE PERSONAL WORKER HIMSELF — HIS QUALIFICATIONS.

1. He must be a thorough Christian.

THE first step in bringing other men to Christ is to know the way to Him yourself. In Luke 22:32, Jesus says to Peter: "And when thou art converted, strengthen thy brethren." Peter himself must first be right with God before he can bring others into a right relationship with God.

Although God has in the past, and still does at present, allow even ungodly people to speak the word of life to perishing souls, as for example, unconverted ministers,—thereby making even the wrath of men to praise Him,—yet such cases are merely exceptions to the rule. Generally, one must be a thorough Christian himself before he can be instrumental in leading anxious souls to a seeking Saviour. "First cast out the beam out of thine own eye; and then shalt thou see clearly to cast out the mote out of thy brother's eye" (Matt. 7:5).

2. He must be a Spirit-filled man.

The Spirit of God must have control of his affections. He must live, move and have being in the Spirit. He must trust Him for guidance and direction.

Philip the evangelist is a good illustration of this thought. In Acts 8:29 we find these words: "Then the Spirit said unto Philip, Go near, and join thyself to this chariot." Philip was obedient to the promptings of the Spirit, and in the 30th verse we read "And

Philip ran thither to him." He might have said what Moses did,—"Lord, send someone else." "Lord, I cannot speak to this stranger. I have never had an introduction to him. He may not care for my company." Some of us would have said that; but Philip was obedient to the promptings of the Holy Spirit, and did just what the Spirit commanded him to do, asking no questions. The Bible says, "Philip ran to him," indicating his swift obedience.

Are you willing to speak to those around you about their soul's eternal welfare?—to those who sit at the same table with you, and who abide under the same roof with you? Mother, father, has the Spirit never said to you: "Go join thyself to your child, and teach him or her the way of salvation?" Yes, but you have not obeyed. Knowest thou the awful responsibility resting upon thee? Read Ezekiel 3:17-19.

Listen! hark! they are calling the roll in heaven. Mother, where is your child? Father, where are your children? Young man, young woman, where are your friends? "While you are busy here and there, they are gone." While you are busy seeking after the things of earth, your children have slipped between your fingers, you have no more spiritual influence over them; they are lost! Read 1 Kings 20:39,40.

3. He must be a man of prayer.

It was while Peter was praying that he received the prompting of the Spirit to go to Cornelius and tell him what to do to be saved. "I was in the city of Joppa praying: and in a trance I saw a vision, A certain vessel descend, as it had been a great sheet, let down from heaven by four corners; and it came even to me . . . . . And the Spirit bade me go with them, nothing doubting. Moreover these six brethren accompanied me, and we entered into the man's house" (Acts 11:5, 12.)

(a) We must pray that God will lead us to the right person.

I do not think it is necessary for us, nor do I think God expects us, to speak to every person we see about his soul's salvation. We have not the time for that. I do believe, however, that, as the Spirit led Philip to go and join himself to a certain (this) chariot, so the Spirit of God will give us, in answer to prayer, the inward prompting, so that we may know when to speak and to whom.

(b) We must pray also that God will enable us to speak the right words.

We must ask Him to give the Word power; for we must not forget, that though Paul may plant and Apollos water, yet it is God that must give the increase (1 Cor. 3:6).

(c) Then we must *pray that God will continue the work* already begun in the heart of the person with whom we have spoken.

And right here we may learn from the Apostle Paul, who never forgot to remember his converts in prayer after he had left them (Eph. 1:16-20; Phil. 1:4. 5; Col. 1:3, 4).

4. He must have a desire to see souls saved.

The secret of success is here. Christ had a burning love for souls. Listen to Him as He stands on the mount overlooking the Holy City, and saying: "O Jerusalem, Jerusalem, thou that killest the prophets, and stonest them which are sent unto thee, how often would I have gathered thy children together, even as a hen gathereth her chickens under her wings, and ye would not" (Matt. 23:37). "And when he was come near, he beheld the city, and wept over it" (Luke 19:41).

Have you ever wept over souls? "No," you say; "I have never felt the burden of souls heavy enough for that; how may I feel the weight of souls?" Consider the value of a soul; what it cost; what a sacrifice was made to redeem it; its capabilities; its eternal destiny to glory or despair; that you are in a very real sense your brother's keeper, and then ask God to make you feel the mighty importance of trying to rescue some perishing soul as a brand plucked from the burning.

Paul had a passionate love for souls. He says: "I have great heaviness and continual sorrow in my heart. For I could wish that myself were accursed (or separated) from Christ for my brethren, my kinsmen according to the flesh" (Rom. 9:2,3). The Apostle Paul's heart broke loose from the prolonged logical argument and poured itself out in one vehement exclamation of love, "I could wish myself accursed for my brethren's sake,"—"accursed," given over to hopeless, eternal death; accursed "from Christ," the joy, the joy of his soul; "accursed," he the loyal one, from his all in all, if only the Israel of his love could be saved!

A man may be a successful physician without having love for his patients; he may be a successful lawyer without having love for his clients; he may be a successful merchant without having love for his patrons: but no man can be a successful co-worker with God without having love for souls, and a longing desire to see them saved.

When John Knox, in the enclosure behind his house, pierced the stillness of the night with the thrice-repeated, intense appeal, "Give me Scotland, or I die!" that eager, yearning, well-nigh broken heart got its Scotland. When Brainerd went to sleep thinking of souls and dreaming dreams of them, and, waking, still thought and prayed for them, souls became his. "Tell me," says Maclaren, "the depth of a Christian man's compassion, and I will tell you the measure of his usefulness. The wealth of Egypt's harvest is proportioned to the depth of the Nile's overflow." Christ, the model Christian worker, is portrayed as "moved with compassion," as though a great surging tide flowed over his heart when he saw the multitudes standing before him in their want.

The power of these great religious leaders of all time, lay deeper than their mighty intellects—it lay in their love for souls.

Souls, souls, souls! I yearn for souls. This is the cry of the Saviour—and to save souls He died upon the cross, and remains until eternity their intercessor.

Souls, souls, souls! This is the cry of Satan—and to obtain them he scatters gold to tempt them, multiplies their wants and pleasures, and gives them praise that only infatuates.

Souls, souls, souls! This must be our one cry and passion, Christian worker; and for the sake of one soul we must be willing to spend and be spent.

5. He must have confidence in the power of, and in, the Word of God.

We do well to heed the Lord's rebuke to Sarah in Gen. 18:14, "Is any thing too hard for the Lord?" No matter how desperate the case may be, God can save to the uttermost. If the person you are seeking to lead to Christ be the "chief of sinners," 1 Tim. 1:15 will suit him:

> This is a faithful saying, and worthy of all acceptation, that Christ Jesus came into the world to save sinners; of whom I am chief.

If he be a murderer, Isa. 1:18 will comfort him:

> Come now, and let us reason together, saith the Lord: though your sins be as scarlet, they shall be as white as snow; though they be red like crimson, they shall be as wool.

If an outcast, Luke 19:10 is just the passage he needs:

> For the Son of man is come to seek and to save that which was lost.

Let us take for our motto, when we are tempted to be discouraged because of the seeming indifference and hardness of those we are seeking to lead to Christ, the following passages of Scripture:

Matt. 19:25, 26:

> When his disciples heard it, they were exceedingly amazed, saying, Who then can be saved? But Jesus beheld them, and said unto them, With men this is impossible; but with God all things are possible.

Job 42:1, 2:

> Then Job answered the Lord, and said,
> I know that thou canst do everything, and that no thought can be withholden from thee.

Isaiah 55:10, 11:

> For as the rain cometh down, and the snow from heaven, and returneth not thither, but watereth the earth, and maketh it bring forth and bud, that it may give seed to the sower, and bread to the eater:
> So shall my word be that goeth forth out of my mouth: it shall not return unto me void, but it shall accomplish that which I please, and it shall prosper in the thing whereto I sent it.

Fourteen hundred years before the birth of Jesus, Baalam, by special inspiration, addressed Balak with these profound words: "God is not a man that he should lie; neither the son of man, that he should repent: hath he said, and shall he not do it? or hath he spoken, and shall he not make it good?" (Num. 23:19.)

Paul the apostle, fifteen hundred years after Baalam, echoes the same testimony: "In hope of eternal life, which God, that cannot lie, promised before the world began" (Titus 1:2). Let us trust confidently in the Word and promises of God.

An illustration will show more plainly what I mean: A Christian worker once met a man who was hardened in sin and skepticism. After speaking to him about becoming a Christian, he said: "I do not believe in the Bible, or in God, or in heaven or hell. I am a skeptic." The worker took no notice of the man's confession, but quoted to him this passage: "Except ye repent, ye shall all likewise perish" (Luke 13:3). "But," he said again, "did I not tell you I did not believe in the Bible? why do you quote it to me?" The Christian again quoted the same verse, and again the skeptic gave the same reply. After repeating that same verse, adding no words of his own to it, about a dozen times, the worker said to him, "Now, my friend, I do not remember half of what you have said to me; but you cannot forget the passage of Scripture I have quoted to you, and I am going to pray that God will, through that passage of Scripture, and His Holy Spirit, cause you to realize its truth." "But," he continued, "I do not believe it." Then was quoted Romans 3:3, 4: "For what if some did not believe? shall their unbelief make the faith of God without effect? God forbid," etc. The Christian then left the skeptic in the hands of God.

The next night the skeptic sought him and confessed that he had spent a miserable night. He said: "That verse you quoted so often has haunted me ever since; it will not leave my memory. Won't you show me how to find rest for my soul?" What a joy it was to point him to John 1:29, leave him in Acts 13:52, and commend him to Jude 24. Thus, you see, God will honor His own Word.

INSTRUCTIONS TO
THE SOUL-WINNER

CHAPTER IV.

INSTRUCTIONS TO THE SOUL - WINNER.

1. Who can engage in this work of personal soul-winning?

FORTUNATELY, no Christian, however insignificant he may feel himself to be, or however limited his talents, is shut out from the opportunity of soul-winning. Inasmuch as God holds all Christians responsible for this work, it must be possible for all to do it. Aquila and Priscilla (Acts 18:26-28) are good illustrations of the opportunities that are afforded every *individual* Christian. Philip (Acts 8) and Paul (Acts 20:31) show us how *preachers* may engage in this work. 2 Kings 5:1-5 tells of a *housemaid* doing this kind of work. It is said that Lord Shaftesbury was led to Christ through one of his housemaids. John 1 gives a picture of a *teacher* leading his *pupil* (v. 29) ; a *brother,* his brother (vs. 40, 41) ; and a *friend,* his friend (vs. 43-45) to Christ as the Saviour of the world. 2 Timothy 1:5 and 3:15 afford us a splendid example for *parents* to lead their children to Christ.

Every Christian should be a personal worker for Christ just as every sinner is a worker for Satan. No one is excluded from this great work.

2. Where may personal soul-winning be done?

Is there any place in which it cannot be done? is a more fitting way to put it. Jesus did it in the temple, in the streets, on the seaside, in a boat, on the mountain-side, and in the house.

Mr. Moody, who was perhaps the greatest personal soul-winner of his day, made it a practice of his life to speak to men on the street-cars. In thus dealing with a man in a Detroit street-car, he asked him the question: "Are you a Christian?" The man answered: "No, sir; but I wish I were." Mr. Moody there and then led the man to Christ.

According to Oriental thought and custom, one with whom you break bread, or with whom you sit at meat is, by that very fact, in covenant with you, and you have sacred duties toward him which must not be shirked or avoided. Has not the Christian similar relations under similar circumstances? Yet how often, yea, rather how seldom, if at all, do we realize these privileges and responsibilities! We talk to friends on other topics, such as politics, and the weather: why not speak to them of Christ?

Governments have two ways of saving life: the life-saving station and the lighthouse. The rescue mission is the life-saving station and crew; but the ship must be on the rocks, or the man be in the water, before this agency can render help. The Sunday-school is a lighthouse; it warns the ship before it gets onto the rocks. What an opportunity both the rescue mission and the Sunday-school worker have to do personal soul-winning work! Yet how incomparably greater is the opportunity of the Sunday-school teacher. Jesus put a little child in the midst, and he has been in the midst, the center of attraction, ever since; the world revolves around the little child. It is said that on nineteen different occasions Jesus sat down and taught one scholar.

The close of the regular church service affords a splendid opportunity for speaking to souls. Already hearts have in all probability been touched by the preached word, and may be longing to have someone deal definitely with them, and point them individually to Jesus Christ. It was at the close of a great service that Philip won his convert (Acts 8:37, 38).

If you want a field of labor,
You can find one anywhere.

8. How personal soul-winning work may be done.

By the use of the mails. Write letters. Here is a vast and almost unemployed agency for the advancement of the kingdom of God. Dedicate your pen to the work of postal evangelism. A Christian Japanese telegraphed to his brother to come home because of important business. The brother came. He found out that the "important business" was in the nature of a great revival that was then in progress in Tokyo. After some hesitancy he decided to stay at home and attend the meetings. On the last night of the meetings he was converted.

Nothing, however, takes the place of the personal *heart-to-heart, face-to-face* talk. This can be had in the shop, office, store, hall, church, on the street, in the home. Make it your business to talk with your friends about Christ.

Tracts may be effectively used. One day a man riding on a street-car in New York was handed a tract which read, "Look to Jesus when tempted, troubled, or dying!" The man read the tract carefully. As the car reached its destination and the passengers were getting off, he who received the tract said to the man who gave it to him: "Sir, when you gave me this tract, I was on my way down to the river to drown myself. My wife and son have both died, and there is nothing for me to live for. God bless you for giving me this encouraging message." Seventeen hundred people are said to have written to Dr. Chickering, the author of the tract, "What is it to believe on Christ?" stating that they were led to Christ by the use of this leaflet. Many people who may feel themselves too timid to speak a word for Christ, may be thus able to give the word in this manner.

If you have a tract in your possession—and, by the
way, all Christians should carry a supply of evangelistic literature with them ready for such use—you may
give it. Let your friend read the tract, and then ask
him what he thinks of it.

How to Begin.

How to begin a conversation along personal soul-
winning lines is not always easily determined. A sug-
gestion or two in this direction may not be out of place.

*Generally, men should deal with men, and women
with women; the young with the young, and the old
with the old.* This rule applies particularly to adults,
and not to adults dealing with children. Unless it is
absolutely necessary, this rule should not be broken.

*Avoid introducing your subject by an abrupt ques-
tion.* Lead naturally up to the question of the inquirer
becoming a Christian. Jesus, in his dealing with the
Samaritan woman (John 4), and Philip (Acts 8) are
good examples to follow. To begin by asking at once:
"Are you a Christian?" or "Are you saved?" or some
such question may, in exceptional cases, be effective,
but usually such an approach antagonizes. It is better, especially if you have time enough to do it, to
begin on some other topic and gradually lead up to
the question of the acceptance of Christ. Philip asked,
"Understandest thou what thou readest?" (Acts 8:30).
Christ spoke to the Samaritan woman on the general
subject of water to begin with (John 4:7).

If you should be dealing with the inquirer at the
close of a sermon or service, you may introduce your
subject by asking him how he liked the sermon, etc.

*Get the inquirer alone, and do not allow yourself,
if you can prevent it, to be interrupted.* The presence
of a third person is usually fatal to the effectiveness of
personal work with souls. Often an inquirer who has

been opening his heart to the worker has closed it at once as a third person has appeared. As a general rule, no one is convinced in the presence of a crowd; certainly no man will unbosom himself to a spiritual adviser in the presence of others.

To be interrupted while dealing with an inquirer is ofttimes disastrous. Some well-meaning but poorly instructed people seem to find delight in seeking to encourage the inquirer and the worker by saying: "Oh, yes, my friend, what the worker is saying is true; do believe it; we are praying for you," or some such words. To do this may be fatal. The worker may have been dealing with the inquirer along a certain line of thought until he is at the point of yielding. For some one not acquainted with this method to come and ignorantly interrupt the conversation may be to neutralize all that the worker has thus far done. Do not interrupt others; do not allow others to interrupt you.

Aim to bring about a decision as soon as you can. Get the inquirer on his knees at the earliest possible moment. This posture of the body has much more to do with the element of submission on the part of the will than we think. As a rule, the bended knee is the end of all argument.

Emphasize the immediate acceptance of Jesus Christ as personal Saviour. Do not be content until the inquirer has definitely settled his personal relationship to Jesus Christ. As many as receive Him become children of God. To receive Christ as personal Saviour is the all-important thing. It is not enough to answer the inquirer's questions, to dissolve his doubts, or to enlighten his ignorance. All this the worker may do and still leave the man unsaved. To leave the inquirer with the question of the acceptance of Jesus Christ as his personal Saviour settled—this is the aim and end of all personal dealing.

Do not enter into a heated argument. Men are not usually convinced by this method of dealing. "The servant of the Lord must not strive" (2 Tim. 2:23, 24). Hold yourself well in hand. Keep your poise; control yourself; do not lose your temper; be courteous at all times and under all circumstances. Remember Jesus Christ—how graciously He received the contradiction of sinners. When He was reviled, He reviled not again. Do thou likewise.

Be courageous. Do not fear the face of man. Remember that in spiritual matters the Christian worker possesses the confidence that comes from a settled conviction of a right relation to God. The sinner does not possess this, and consequently does not have the courage that issues from it. The sinner is the fearful one; the Christian is bold and courageous. Some Christians, however, are naturally timid, and, therefore, find it an almost impossible task to approach people in this way. We would recommend to such for their consideration the case of Peter and his timidity (or cowardice) before Pentecost (Mark 14:66-72), and Peter and his courage after Pentecost (Acts 2:14). We would also suggest that the prayer of the early Christians for courage be pondered and appropriated (Acts 4:23-31).

Get the inquirer to read for himself the verses you use in dealing with him. It makes a much deeper impression upon his mind if he sees and reads the Scriptures for himself. Christian workers of the longest and largest experience particularly emphasize this point.

Looking at the great number of Scripture references in this volume, it would seem like asking something that was impossible, to suggest the memorizing of them all. Yet it is a comparatively easy task if undertaken in the right manner.

A few suggestions will be helpful here.

1. Memorize the location of the verse together with the verse. You will find it just as easy to say, "John 1:29, Behold the Lamb of God, which taketh away the sin of the world," as you would if you merely said, "Behold the Lamb of God," etc., omitting to state the reference.

2. Learn it. Don't get a faint, indefinite idea. If you want to remember any text in after years, let it make a deep, clear and vivid impression on your mind the moment you learn it.

3. Read the verse over, say twenty times; close your Bible and see if you can repeat it correctly, then to be sure, read it again. Once writing the verse is worth a dozen repetitions of it by mouth.

4. Review. This is the secret of memorizing. Review every day, every week, every month, and every year.

5. Practice. Use the passages of Scripture. Seek occasions for talking to persons who have difficulties.

The writer's book entitled, *How to Memorize*, issued by the publishers of this work, will be found very helpful in memorizing any matter, but especially the Scriptures.

THE UNINTERESTED
AND UNCONCERNED

CHAPTER V.

I. THE UNINTERESTED AND UNCONCERNED.

HOW shall we treat those with whom we speak concerning their spiritual condition, and for whose salvation we are anxious, who nevertheless treat our approaches and earnest solicitations with seeming contempt, or, to say the least, with apparent indifference? Our best efforts, our most prayerful pleadings, seem not to move them. They remain not only unmoved, but uninterested. To us they seem to be an unreasonable and a gainsaying people. Such persons may be among our most intimate friends, members of our families, husband or wife, brother or sister. The thought of their being lost is more than we can bear. Yet we do not seem to be able to interest them in the salvation of their own souls. What shall we say? what can we do? what arguments can we bring forth that shall, under God, be the means of bringing them to realize their need of Christ as their personal Saviour?

We must not treat all men alike, any more than a physician treats all people alike who come to him for medical attention. Jude 22, 23 suggests a difference of method in dealing with souls—"And of some have compassion, making a difference: and others save with fear, pulling them out of the fire."

There are four general ways in which we may deal with the Uninterested and Unconcerned:

1. Under "fear."—Aim to produce a conviction of sin.

All men need to be brought face to face with the fact that they have sinned, for without this knowledge there can hardly be any heartfelt need of a Saviour.

Of course, it is the work of the Holy Spirit to produce conviction of sin (John 16:9). No human teacher, no Christian worker, however faithful and consecrated, can produce it; conscience cannot produce it; even the Gospel itself cannot do it. Although the Word of God is the sword of the Spirit, yet, unless the Spirit of God draws forth and wields that sword, it lies powerless in its scabbard. Only when He wields it, is it "quick and powerful" (Heb. 4:12). The power is from God. Yet man is the instrument: it is the "sword of the Lord, and of Gideon," too.

Now, what scriptures shall we use to produce conviction of sin? Through the law is the knowledge of sin. "I had not known sin, but by the law" (Rom. 7:7). A man must acknowledge himself to be a sinner before he can call on God for forgiveness. Therefore—

(a) Use such passages of Scripture as are likely to produce conviction of sin.

First, the fact of sin. Show the inquirer that he has sinned, that he is a sinner. To do this, use:

Isa. 53:6:

> All we like sheep have gone astray; we have turned every one to his own way; and the Lord hath laid on him the iniquity of us all.

Rom. 3:10, 23:

> There is none righteous, no, not one;
> For all have sinned and come short of the glory of God.

Show that "all" includes him. We may differ in the extent but not in the nature of sin. All have gone astray from God. If the inquirer says he has not sinned, show him 1 John 1:8, 10. To say we have not sinned is to make God a liar. But God is true. He is "not a man that he should lie." "Let God be true, but every man a liar" (Rom. 3:4).

It is possible that the inquirer may say, in this connection: "Well, I have not sinned much; I am not a great sinner." Ask him what is his definition of a great sinner. He will doubtless say, "One who has broken much of the law." You may then read to him Matt. 22 :37, 38 :

> Jesus said unto him, Thou shalt love the Lord thy God with all thy heart, and with all thy soul, and with all thy mind.
> This is the first and great commandment.

Ask him if he has loved God in the manner indicated in this verse—with all the heart, mind, soul, strength? Show him just what it means to thus love God; that we must love Him supremely, and put the doing of His will before all else. If he speaks the truth, he will confess that he has not thus loved God. Then ask him what commandment he has broken: "The first and the greatest." If a man breaks the greatest commandment, is he not a great sinner? Then, again, to intensify the thought of sin, James 2 :10 may be used :

> For whosoever shall keep the whole law, and yet offend in one point, he is guilty of all.

Show him from this passage that to break one commandment is to break them all. Therefore, according to his own definition of a great sinner, he is such a sinner, inasmuch as he has broken the whole law.

(b) Use such passages as set forth the consequences of sin.

Inasmuch as the inquirer has just admitted that he has not kept "the whole law," it is well to show him from Gal. 3 :10 the penalty God has attached to such disobedience.

> For as many as are of the works of the law are under the curse: for it is written, Cursed is every one that continueth not in all things which are written in the book of the law to do them.

The law demands a perfect and a continual obedience, and the man who fails to render such an obedience is "under the curse"; that is to say, he is separated and banished from God. The pronouncement of woe has already been passed upon him. He is "already condemned"; compare Rom. 6:23; Ezek. 18:4.

Sometimes the objector will say, "I shall be glad to die, for then there will be an end to all my trouble." You may then show him that "death," in the Bible meaning of the word, does not denote cessation of existence, but, on the contrary, an endless conscious existence. To prove this, use:

Rev. 21:8:

> But the fearful, and unbelieving, and the abominable, and murderers, and whoremongers, and sorcerers, and idolaters, and all liars, shall have their part in the lake which burneth with fire and brimstone: which is the second death.

Also Rev. 14:10, 11; John 3:36 and 8:21, 24 to show that continuance in sin will shut the gate of heaven in a man's face, and bring down upon him the perpetual wrath of God.

It has been objected to this method of dealing with men, that it is making an appeal on the ground of fear, which is unworthy and low. Suffice it to say in reply that we are conscious of no cowardice in thus appealing to the element of fear. Our Master appealed to it again and again. More than once did he refer to the worm that dieth not and the fire that shall never be quenched. If men will not respond to the higher motive of love, there is then nothing else for us to do than to appeal to the lower motive of fear. We must "by all means save some." If Mount Calvary will not melt the heart of the sinner, then we must take him to Mount Sinai, that it may be broken into penitence.

(c) Particularly should the guilt of rejecting Christ as the Saviour be shown.

Men do not realize as they should the enormity of the guilt of rejecting Jesus Christ. Yet unbelief is the greatest sin in the world. It is not generally recognized as such; possibly because it is a state rather than an act, and has no outward form as has the committal of some other sins, murder or adultery, for instance. Yet the sin of unbelief is the condemning sin of the world. It is the office of the Holy Spirit to convict men of this specific sin. To show the greatness of this sin use:

John 3:17-19:

> For God sent not his Son into the world to condemn the world; but that the world through him might be saved.
> He that believeth on him is not condemned; but he that believeth not is condemned already, because he hath not believed in the name of the only begotten Son of God.
> And this is the condemnation, that light is come into the world, and men loved darkness rather than light, because their deeds were evil.

Note the context: Christ came not into the world to ruin it, but to save it. A man abandons himself to ruin by the rejection of Jesus Christ.

Hebrews 10:28, 29 shows the awful punishment awaiting those who reject the redemptive work of Jesus Christ.

> He that despised Moses' law died without mercy under two or three witnesses:
> Of how much sorer punishment, suppose ye, shall he be thought worthy, who hath trodden under foot the Son of God, and hath counted the blood of the covenant, wherewith he was sanctified, an unholy thing, and hath done despite unto the Spirit of grace?

The more clearly God's will is made known, the greater the guilt in resisting it. The revelation of God in Christ is greater by far than the revelation of God in the law (Heb. 2:2). God's will has been fully made known in Christ, hence the guilt of rejecting Him.

By using Hebrews 2:3 with 12:25 we learn that those who disobeyed the revelation of God as given by angels did not escape the punishment of God; how much less "shall we escape, if we neglect so great salvation," which was spoken by our Lord?

2. **Under "love."**—Use scriptures that set forth God's love in giving His Son, Jesus Christ. Seek to awaken the inquirer's gratitude to God for His unspeakable gift.

John 3:16 sets forth in a wondrous way the love of God to man:

> For God so loved the world, that he gave his only begotten Son, that whosoever believeth in him should not perish, but have everlasting life.

Many a time the mere reading of this verse has melted the soul of a hardened sinner to tears. The reading of the nineteenth chapter of John—the story of the crucifixion of Christ—if read carefully and prayerfully—will often break up the fountains of the deep of the sinner's heart and reveal to him the wondrous love of Christ for him.

Isa. 53:4, 5:

> Surely he hath borne our griefs, and carried our sorrows: yet we did esteem him stricken, smitten of God, and afflicted.
> But he was wounded for our transgressions, he was bruised for our iniquities: the chastisement of our peace was upon him; and with his stripes we are healed.

It is a good thing, in reading this passage, to change the pronoun "our" into "my," and thus make the matter more personal: "He was wounded for *my* transgressions, He was bruised for *my* iniquities."

Rom. 2:4:

> Or despisest thou the riches of his goodness and forbearance and longsuffering; not knowing that the goodness of God leadeth thee to repentance?

What a magnificent opportunity to dwell upon the goodness of God towards the sinner—His longsuffering, patience, sparing his life in spite of his frequent sinning, etc. Such goodness ought to lead men to repent of their sins and turn unto God.

Here are some incentives given in testimony by some thoughtful Christians setting forth the reasons why they came to Christ:

"Fear set me to thinking, but love led me to decide."
"The love of Jesus as of One who loved me and took care of me."
"His personal love towards me."
"John 3:16."
"The prayer in Gethsemane."
"Because He first loved me."

3. Under "hope."—Appeal to the element of hope which lies deeply hidden in every man's nature.

In Romans 8:24 we are told that "We are saved by hope." This is a legitimate appeal. Christ appealed to the element of hope in the heart of the Samaritan woman when He said: "If thou knewest the gift of God . . . . thou wouldest have asked" (John 4:10). He held out the hope of heaven to the rich young ruler as an inducement to follow Him (Matt. 19:21). It was this element of hope that determined the choice of Moses, for "he had respect unto the recompense of reward" (Heb. 11:26, R. V.).

The Christian worker, therefore, will do well to seek to create an interest in the things of the Christian faith. This may be done in a general way by using 1 Tim. 4:8:

> For bodily exercise profiteth little: but godliness is profitable unto all things, having promise of the life that now is, and of that which is to come.

This passage teaches us that there are present advantages, as well as future blessings, in being a Christian. Then show the inquirer some of the blessings of the Christian life, the which, you may be very sure, he does not possess, but which he can have the moment he becomes a Christian. Let it be remembered here by the worker that not one of the blessings we are now going to mention is possessed by the sinner. He may claim that he does possess them; but the worker, believing the Word of God rather than the word of man, believes the truth that the sinner is destitute of these things. He must also remember, that, deep down in the heart of man, there is a longing desire to possess these blessings. Here are some of the things the sinner may have, if he believes on Christ:

First, *he may know that his sins are all forgiven.*

How much many men would really give to be assured of this fact!

Use Acts 10:43:

> To him give all the prophets witness, that through his name whosoever believeth in him shall receive remission of sins.

Ask him if he would not like to have the assurance that his sins are all forgiven, blotted out, pardoned; that the sin question is forever settled; that there is no longer any barrier between him and God. He doubt less will reply in the affirmative. You can then read this passage again to him, and tell him this blessing may be his, if he will accept Jesus Christ as his own personal Saviour. 1 John 1:9 may be used in the same way.

Second, *the blessing of peace.*

No wicked man has peace. The Word of God distinctly says so.

Isa. 57:20, 21:

> But the wicked are like the troubled sea, when it cannot rest, whose waters cast up mire and dirt.
> There is no peace, saith my God, to the wicked.

The sinner may dispute the Bible and tell you that he has peace, but do not believe him. I remember well dealing with a man along this very line. He was living in sin, and yet claimed to have peace of soul. I quoted the above mentioned passage to him, but he still persisted in saying that he had peace. I said to him, "My friend, it is merely a question of believing you or God; whom shall I believe?" After a few moments he said, "Believe God's Word, for the fact of the matter is I am the most restless man on the face of the earth." I then had him read for himself John 14:27:

> Peace I leave with you, my peace I give unto you: not as the world giveth, give I unto you. Let not your heart be troubled, neither let it be afraid.

Isa. 26:3:

> Thou wilt keep him in perfect peace, whose mind is stayed on thee: because he trusteth in thee.

Third, *The blessing of fellowship with God.*
1 John 1:3:

> That which we have seen and heard declare we unto you, that ye also may have fellowship with us: and truly our fellowship is with the Father, and with his Son Jesus Christ.

These and many other blessings which the acceptance of Christ brings with it may be dealt with further in detail as the circumstances in the case may determine.

4. **Under "altruism."**—Sometimes the desire to be a blessing to others leads a person to accept the Saviour.

Here are some of the expressions I have personally gathered from the testimony of Christian workers: "I wanted to engage in the Lord's work of winning souls, but I knew I could not unless I became a Christian." "God's need of laborers." "To keep from being a stumbling-block to others." "To do something for the lost." "The thought of being able to help others." "The feeling which I had that I ought to do something for others, and for Christ." "I wanted to be of some good in the world." "To make my life count for something." These are the expressed reasons why these young men gave themselves to Jesus Christ. Why should we not, therefore, say to men, that they can do good in the world, be of much service to God and their fellowmen if they become Christians? The argument that a man may do good may be much more effective with him in leading him to Christ, than the presentation of the truth that much good will come to him personally by so doing. The appeal to Hobab (Num. 10:29-32), "Come thou with us, and we will do thee good," did not win; but the other argument, "Thou mayest be unto us instead of eyes," won. Jesus said: "For their sakes I sanctify myself" (John 17:19).

Daniel 12:3:

> And they that be wise shall shine as the brightness of the firmament; and they that turn many to righteousness as the stars for ever and ever.

James 5:20 may be used in the same way:

> Let him know, that he which converteth the sinner from the error of his way shall save a soul from death, and shall hide a multitude of sins.

THOSE WHO ARE INTERESTED
AND CONCERNED, BUT IGNO-
RANT OF THE WAY OF LIFE

CHAPTER VI.

II. THOSE WHO ARE INTERESTED AND CON-CERNED, BUT IGNORANT OF THE WAY OF LIFE.

THERE are many seeking after God who do not know the way to Him. Like the Ethiopian eunuch, they are interested and concerned about the way of life, and say with him, "How can I know the way, except someone show me?" More than one soul is, at this very minute, crying out, "O that I knew where I might find Him! I go forward, but He is not there; and backward, but I cannot perceive Him; on the left hand where He doth work, but I cannot behold Him; He hideth Himself on the right hand, that I cannot see Him." Like the Philippian jailer, many are convinced of their sin, and cry out, "What shall I do to be saved?" Happy indeed is that Christian worker who, like Philip and Paul, can "find the place where it is written * * * Believe on the Lord Jesus Christ, and thou shalt be saved."

A splendid illustration of one who is interested and concerned in the salvation of his soul, but ignorant of what to do to be saved, is found in Cornelius in Acts 10 and 11. He was desirous of becoming a Christian, but was ignorant of the way until the Lord sent Peter unto him to tell him words whereby he might be saved.

WHAT TO DO TO BECOME A CHRISTIAN.

1. Show the inquirer that he must repent.

Repentance is the first step into the kingdom. It is useless to discuss here which comes first—repentance, faith, regeneration, etc. The inquiry room is not a theological clinic or a seminary class-room. It is no place for hair-splitting definitions and relations. So far as the purpose of leading the inquirer to Christ is concerned, repentance comes first: "Ye repented not * * * that ye might believe" (Matt. 21:32).

Use Isa. 55:7:

> Let the wicked forsake his way, and the unrighteous man his thoughts: and let him return unto the Lord, and he will have mercy upon him; and to our God, for he will abundantly pardon.

Use also Acts 26:20; 2 Chron. 7:14.

These passages show that the first thing that God requires of a man who desires to become a Christian is that he repent. There is no conversion without repentance.

It may be necessary to show what repentance is. For this purpose use Psalm 38:6, 18:

> I am troubled; I am bowed down greatly; I go mourning all the day long.
> For I will declare mine iniquity; I will be sorry for my sin.

Use also 2 Cor. 7:9, 10; Matt. 26:75.

These scriptures show that a deep, pungent, heartfelt sorrow for sin is an essential element in repentance.

Men need to mourn because of their sin. Godly sorrow is that which is wrought in the soul by the Spirit of God as man catches a glimpse of the awfulness and the guilt of his sin. It may not be necessary to shed an abundance of tears, but there must be a real heart-sorrow. If Christ wept over the sin of others, surely we ought to weep over our own sins.

Repentance involves the confession of sin. Like David, we must say: "I have sinned, and done this evil in thy sight." The Psalmist not only said: "I will be sorry for my sin," but also "I will declare my iniquity."

Use 1 John 1:9:

> If we confess our sins, he is faithful and just to forgive us our sins, and to cleanse us from all unrighteousness.

Use also Psalm 32:5; Luke 18:13.

God cannot forgive my sin until I confess it to Him. If I do confess, then His promise is, "He is faithful and just to forgive." It is a good thing to get the inquirer to be specific in his confession. General confessions are good; but the confession of particular sins, as well as of sin as a whole, is better. Say with David: "I have done *this* evil in Thy sight." (Compare Dan. 9:3-11.)

Attention ought to be drawn to the fact that there should be confession to man also, if man has been wronged in the sinning.

Use Matt. 5:23, 24:

> Therefore if thou bring thy gift to the altar, and there rememberest that thy brother hath aught against thee;
> Leave there thy gift before the altar, and go thy way; first be reconciled to thy brother, and then come and offer thy gift.

Use also Matt. 6:14, 15; Luke 19:8.

Too often is this truth overlooked in our dealings with men. We must see to it that men are right with man as well as with God. "If a man say, I love God, and hateth his brother, he is a liar: for he that loveth not his brother whom he hath seen, how can he love God whom he hath not seen?" (1 John 4:20.)

Repentance involves a forsaking of sin.

No repentance is real that does not lead a man to forsake his sin. Repentance is not only a heart broken for sin; it is also a heart broken from sin. Until a man has turned away from his sinful ways, he has not truly repented, no matter how loud his pretensions thereto may be.

Use Prov. 28:13:

> He that covereth his sins shall not prosper: but whoso confesseth and forsaketh them shall have mercy.

Use also Isa. 55:7; Ezek. 33:11.

2. Show the inquirer that he must have faith in order to be saved.

He must not only repent, he must "repent, and believe the Gospel." Indeed, repentance is in order to faith: "Ye repented not afterward, that ye might believe" (Matt. 21:32).

There must be faith in the Lord Jesus Christ as the Saviour from the guilt and power of sin.

Use Isa. 53:6:

> All we like sheep have gone astray; we have turned every one to his own way; and the Lord hath laid on him the iniquity of us all.

Also Gal. 3:13; 2 Cor. 5.21; 1 Pet. 2:24.

In these passages we have Christ presented to us as God's sacrificial lamb bearing the sin of the world, charged by God to carry the burden of the world's iniquity. The wrath due our sin was made to strike upon Him; the curse due our sin was borne by Him in His own body on the tree. It was "instead of us" that He suffered and died. "He was made sin for us," in order that we, by accepting His finished work, "might be made the righteousness of God in Him." This is, to say the least, a vital part of the content of saving faith. A man must believe this in order to be saved.

Not only are these facts to be believed, but Jesus Himself is to be *received* as a personal Saviour. Only thus does a man become a child of God by a legitimate right derived from a competent source. This truth is brought out in John 1:12:

> But as many as received him, to them gave he power to become the sons of God, even to them that believe on his name.

That is to say, as many as, accepting Him *(i. e.,* acknowledging His claims as Saviour and King), received Him as such, became, thereby, sons of God. First, I believe His claims, and then I receive Him to be all He claims to be—my personal Saviour and Lord. Thus believing and receiving I am saved.

8. Show the inquirer that he must confess Jesus Christ before the world.

Faith without confession is no more faith than confession without faith is real confession. Salvation may be forfeited by an unwillingness to confess Christ. If faith does not grow into confession, it dies back, first into mere opinion, and then into unbelief. To confess Christ is a test of the reality of our faith in Him; for it is written: "Whosoever believeth on Him shall not be ashamed."

Use Rom. 10:9-11:

> That if thou shalt confess with thy mouth the Lord Jesus, and shalt believe in thine heart that God hath raised him from the dead, thou shalt be saved.
> For with the heart man believeth unto righteousness; and with the mouth confession is made unto salvation.
> For the scripture saith, Whosoever believeth on him shall not be ashamed.

Note, in using this passage, how that, in a sense, salvation hinges upon the confession of Christ. "If * * *, thou shalt be saved." Use also Matt. 10: 32, 33; Mark 10:38.

Ask, "Who is it that is going to be confessed before the Father and the angels in heaven?" The answer will be, "Those who confess Christ here on earth." Then ask, "Whom will Christ deny in heaven?" The text gives the answer: Those who were ashamed to confess Christ here on earth. From this it is clear that, if a man would be a Christian, he must be willing to confess Jesus Christ before the world.

4. Show the inquirer that Christ must be received as Lord and King.

It is not enough to receive Jesus Christ as Saviour from the guilt of sin; He must be received as the director and controller of our life. From henceforth, the Christian must say, "It is no longer I that live, but Christ that liveth in me. Christ, not I, is the Master of my life. From henceforth all that is done must be done with His approval."

Acts 2:36:

> Therefore let all the house of Israel know assuredly, that God hath made that same Jesus, whom ye have crucified, both Lord and Christ.

Col. 3:17:

> And whatsoever ye do in word or deed, do all in the name of the Lord Jesus, giving thanks to God and the Father by him.

See also John 2:5.

THOSE WHO ARE INTERESTED
AND ANXIOUS TO BECOME
CHRISTIANS, BUT HAVE DIF-
FICULTIES IN THE WAY

CHAPTER VII.

III. THOSE WHO ARE INTERESTED AND ANXIOUS TO BECOME CHRISTIANS, BUT HAVE DIFFICULTIES IN THE WAY.

WITH some people there are certain difficulties and obstacles which seem to stand in the way of an acceptance of Christ as Saviour and Lord. These difficulties must be solved—at least those that are solvable—and the obstacles removed. It is the business of the Christian worker, in co-operation with the Holy Spirit, to render this service. The incident of the raising of Lazarus from the dead may serve to illustrate what we here have in mind. Between the life-giving Christ and the dead body of Lazarus there lies a huge stone. Christ has only to speak the word, and, moved by hands irresistible, that stone moves away to reveal the secrets of the tomb. But Christ does not speak that word, nor does He address the stone. He addresses those standing around—to them He says: "Roll ye away the stone." They must do what they can; what they cannot do, He will do. So is it with us in our dealing with souls that are dead in sin: we may not be able to speak the word that shall mean life from the dead, but we can endeavor to remove the obstacles which impede their coming to Him who is the Life. To remove these obstacles, to answer these objections, and to solve these difficulties is not, however, the main purpose of the Christian worker. He does these things simply to bring the sinner into contact with the Saviour. Following are some of the difficulties, objections, and excuses:

1. "I feel that I have sinned too greatly to be forgiven."

How shall we deal with this difficulty? Admit the fact that the inquirer has sinned greatly. Do not minimize sin; there is too little deep conviction of sin nowadays. This may be the reason why there are so many sham conversions. A man will not appreciate Christ as a Saviour until he realizes that he himself is a sinner. He that is forgiven much will love much.

Endeavor next to show from the Scriptures that no sin is too great to be forgiven, if there is penitence and confession. Use the following passages:

1 Tim. 1:15:

> This is a faithful saying, and worthy of all accepta-
> tion, that Christ Jesus came into the world to save
> sinners; of whom I am chief.

Ask the question: "Whom did Jesus Christ come into the world to save?" The answer will be, "Sinners." "Only sinners?" "No, the chief of sinners." "Do you feel that you are a sinner?" "Yes, indeed, the chief of sinners." Then you can show him that he is just the one Jesus Christ came into the world to save.

Romans 5:6-8:

> For when we were yet without strength, in due time
> Christ died for the ungodly.
> For scarcely for a righteous man will one die: yet
> peradventure for a good man some would even dare to die.
> But God commendeth his love toward us, in that,
> while we were yet sinners, Christ died for us.

These verses state that Christ died not for the right-eousness of saints, but for the unrighteousness of sinners. A "righteous" man is one who keeps the law; a "good" man is one who does more than keep the law—he gives "good measure, pressed down, running over." The one "without strength" is the one who is without the ability to do what he knows to be right.

Now, when we were neither "righteous" nor "good," but, on the contrary, when we were weak and ungodly, Christ died for us. The righteous man demands our respect; the good man, our love. When we deserved neither love nor respect, Christ died for us. Christ died for sinners.

Matthew 9:12, 13:

> But when Jesus heard that, he said unto them, They that be whole need not a physician, but they that are sick.
> But go ye and learn what that meaneth, I will have mercy, and not sacrifice: for I am not come to call the righteous, but sinners to repentance.

Read the context. Recall with what ignominy and shame the publicans were regarded. Show from Christ's acceptance of this publican's invitation His attitude toward great sinners. Verses 12 and 13 are Christ's defense of his action, and at the same time show us the purpose of His coming into the world—"not to call the righteous, but sinners to repentance."

Luke 19:10:

> For the Son of man is come to seek and to save that which was lost.

This passage distinctly tells us that Christ left His home in the glory to save whom? "The lost." The inquirer claims to be a lost sinner, therefore he is just the one Jesus Christ came to save.

2. Those who say: "I have no feeling; I do not feel as though I want to be a Christian."

This is a large and a difficult class to deal with. The question of emotion in religion is an intricate one. Leading psychologists have spent much time debating the question pro and con. There still remains much diversity of opinion on the subject. After all, the degree of emotion in religion must, in the very nature of the case, be determined by the temperament of the individual concerned.

As to the source of this excuse, it may come from exaggerated views of some of the conversions recorded in the Bible; e. g., the Philippian jailer (Acts 16), or Saul of Tarsus (Acts 9). If so, it is well to remind them of the childhood conversion of Timothy (2 Tim. 3), and of John the Baptist, who was filled with the Holy Ghost from his mother's womb (Luke 1:15).

This excuse may arise, in the next place, from the striking testimonies given in church meetings and elsewhere by those who have found Christ as their Saviour. Said one such man sometime ago: "I had a long and bitter experience because of the language of people in testimony meetings. At times, I have felt as though I was not as religious as I ought to be, or rather had no religion whatsoever." Once a man in New England was accosted by Mr. Moody, and being asked if he were a Christian, replied, "No, it hasn't struck me yet." This man was looking for an experience similar to one he had heard a friend of his testify to some months before. He thought it was necessary for him to have a similar experience before he could become a Christian. These people think they will get a peculiar and strange inner purpose, a kind of tugging at their will power by a divine impulse which will suggest what to do and what not to do. There can be no doubt but that considerable emotion is present in some conversions, but certainly not in all; nor are we to consider it to be absolutely necessary to any.

Where in all the Bible is feeling demanded as a requisite to salvation? Did Jesus command it? Did Paul, or John, or Peter? Indeed, by referring to the story of Jacob's deception (Gen. 27), we see the folly of depending upon mere feeling.

Jer. 17:9, 10:

> The heart is deceitful above all things, and desperately wicked: who can know it?
> I the Lord search the heart, I try the reins, even to give every man according to his ways, and according to the fruit of his doings.

This verse may be used to good advantage in this connection. It shows that the human heart is not to be absolutely relied upon in such matters.

It will be helpful to show, that, by the testimony of many living witnesses, salvation may be secured without the kind or amount of feeling some seem to think is necessary. A recent report shows, that, of over 2,000 conversions, only 18 per cent were accompanied with any emotion like the fear of hell, or great trembling because of great sinfulness. And in some of these cases the sorrow was an indefinable something, rather than any clearly defined state of feeling. Indeed, a great proportion of those questioned bore witness to the fact that a sense of sin came really after their conversion. God's order is fact, faith, and then feeling. Satan reverses this order, making feeling first, faith last.

SHOW FROM THE BIBLE WHAT GOD REQUIRES IN ORDER
TO BE SAVED.

(a) Faith. John 1:12:

> But as many as received him, to them gave he power to become the sons of God, even to them that believe on his name.

Also Acts 13:38, 39; John 3:36.

(b) Confession and forsaking of sin.

Prov. 28:13:

> He that covereth his sins shall not prosper: but whose confesseth and forsaketh them shall have mercy.

Also 1 John 1:9; Isa. 55:7.

It might be well to use the method suggested under "The Uninterested and Unconcerned"—such passages as are likely to produce conviction of sin.

3. Those who say, "I am seeking, but I cannot find Christ."

The trouble is, undoubtedly, that they are not seeking God sincerely.

Use Jer. 29:13:

> And ye shall seek me, and find me, when ye shall search for me with all your heart.

Also Rom. 10:6-10; John 12:37-41.

These passages show that it is possible to tell the very moment when a man may find Christ—the very moment he seeks for Him with all the heart. He is not far away from any one of us (Acts 17:27, 28).

You may next show that not only is it true that he is seeking Christ, but also that Christ is seeking him. The parable of the Prodigal Son, and that of the Saviour seeking the Lost Sheep (Luke 15) both illustrate this truth. It ought not to take long for a seeking sinner and the seeking Saviour to meet.

It might be well, seeing he does not know how to seek God properly, to show him how to do so. See Chapter VI, on "Those Who are Interested and Concerned, but Ignorant of the Way of Life."

4. "I would like to be a Christian, but I cannot give up my evil ways."

There are two ways of dealing with this class:

(a) Show them that they are not to depend upon their own strength to give up their sinful ways, but that the power of Christ in their hearts will enable them to overcome all evil.

Phil. 4:13:

> I can do all things through Christ which **strengtheneth** me.

Ezek. 36:25-27:

> Then will I sprinkle clean water upon you, and **ye** shall be clean: from all your filthiness, and from all your idols, will I cleanse you.
>
> A new heart also will I give you, and a new spirit will I put within you: and I will take away the stony heart out of your flesh, and I will give you an heart of flesh.
>
> And I will put my spirit within you, and cause you **to** walk in my statutes, and ye shall keep my judgments, and do them.

Also use 2 Cor. 5:14-17.

The inspiring and strengthening truth prominent in all these passages is that God will put a spirit into our hearts that will enable us to overcome our evil ways; that we are strengthened to live upright when we are in Christ; that we need not fear the power of evil, if we are truly sons of God; that, through faith in God, the impossible becomes possible.

(b) They should be given to understand that they can and they must give up their evil ways or perish.

Gal. 6:7, 8:

> Be not deceived; God is not mocked: for whatsoever a man soweth, that shall he also reap.
>
> For he that soweth to his flesh shall of the flesh reap corruption.

Rom. 2:8, 9:

> But unto them that are contentious, and do not obey the truth, but obey unrighteousness, indignation and wrath,
>
> Tribulation and anguish, upon every soul of man that doeth evil, of the Jew first, and also of the Gentile.

Also use Eccl. 11:8, 9.

5. **"I would like to become a Christian, but it would hurt my business if I did."**

There is much truth in this objection so far as some forms of business are concerned. There are some commodities that no man, Christian or non-Christian, ought to handle, or sell to his fellowmen. This much is most certainly true with regard to some forms of business, that, as soon as a man becomes a Christian, he must forsake them. For example, a Christian saloon-keeper is a contradiction.

It is a comforting thought, however, to know that, in the ordinary, necessary and legitimate lines of business, a man can conduct himself as a Christian man. It must be conceded that there may, and do arise opportunities where a prevarication of the truth, a false representation, or an unrighteous investment promise, and even yield, large financial returns, whereas strict adherence to truth and righteousness would have somewhat lessened the receipts. It is just at this point that the above-named objection becomes important of consideration.

That a man can be a business man and a Christian—this is most certainly true. That a man sometimes loses by loyalty to the Christian standard in business, is also true. That in the end every man who carries Christ into his business dealings comes out gloriously triumphant and successful there can be not the slightest reasonable doubt.

In dealing with this class of excuses we need to make very prominent the great and eternal truth that that "which is seen is temporal—but that which is unseen is eternal"; that "a man's life consisteth not in the abundance of things which he possesseth"; that very often, if not always, in our vain attempt to gain the world, we lose our souls.

The following passages are helpful in dealing with this class:

2 Chron. 25:9:

> And Amaziah said to the man of God, But what shall
> we do for the hundred talents which I have given to
> the army of Israel? And the man of God answered,
> The Lord is able to give thee much more than this.

Mark 10:29, 30:

> And Jesus answered and said, Verily I say unto you,
> There is no man that hath left house, or brethren, or
> sisters, or father, or mother, or wife, or children, or
> lands, for my sake, and the gospel's,
> But he shall receive an hundredfold now in this time,
> houses, and brethren, and sisters, and mothers, and child-
> ren, and lands, with persecutions; and in the world to
> come eternal life.

A saloon-keeper, who was desirous of becoming a
Christian, but who was doubtful of his ability to sup-
port himself and family, if he gave up his business,
was shown these verses. The thought that God was
able to give him much more than he had to give up
for Christ, so strengthened him that he at once relin-
quished his illegitimate business and came out de-
cidedly for Christ.

Mark 8:36:

> For what shall it profit a man, if he shall gain the
> whole world, and lose his own soul?

This verse is a good problem in profit and loss. A
man cannot gain the world and save his soul at the
same time. Which is the wiser thing to do: sacrifice
the salvation of the soul for the paltry gaining of
material things by non-Christian methods, or be honest
in business, be satisfied with a little less, if need be,
and save the soul?

Luke 12:16-21:

> And he spake a parable unto them, saying: The ground
> of a certain rich man brought forth plentifully:
> And he thought within himself, saying, What shall I
> do, because I have no room where to bestow my fruits?
> And he said, This will I do: I will pull down my
> barns, and build greater; and there will I bestow all
> my fruits and my goods.

And I will say to my soul, Soul, thou hast much goods laid up for many years; take thine ease, eat, drink, and be merry.

But God said unto him, Thou fool, this night thy soul shall be required of thee: then whose shall those things be, which thou hast provided?

So is he that layeth up treasure for himself, and is not rich toward God.

The parable of the Rich Fool shows the result of living only for the things of this world, and having no treasure in the world to come. We can carry none of this world's goods into the next world. We leave them for others. We leave the world as we came into it— empty. The only thing that will be of any value to us in the world to come will be what we have done for Christ and in His name.

Matthew 6:33:

But seek ye first the kingdom of God, and his righteousness; and all these things shall be added unto you.

Show the inquirer from this verse that his first duty is to see that his business does not interfere with his religion.

6. **"I would like to be a Christian, but I cannot forgive my enemies."**

(a) Show them that what is seemingly impossible to the natural man is quite possible to the Christian through grace; that God can take away from us a heart filled with hatred and replace it with a heart filled with love.

Ezek. 36:25-27; Mark 9:23.

Phil. 4:13. (See under 4, page 78.)

(b) Show them that unless they forgive their enemies, God will not forgive them.

To have forgiven others is one of the pleas we need to offer to God for our own forgiveness.

Matt. 6:12:

And forgive us our debts, as we forgive our debtors.

The true rendering of this verse is: "And forgive us our debts as we *have* forgiven our debtors." God's forgiveness is conditioned, in a sense, on our having forgiven our enemies.

The parable of the Unmerciful Servant is full of instructive truth along this line of thought. Read it carefully. It is found in Matthew 18:23-35.

He who refuses to forgive those who have wronged him, shuts the door of heaven in his own face. In the eyes of God he is no better than a murderer, and none such shall ever enter the gates of heaven.

1 John 3:15:

Whosoever hateth his brother is a murderer; and ye know that no murderer hath eternal life abiding in him.

This excuse, or more properly, this great sin, is holding more people in its grasp than we have any idea of. It is worthy of note that it is the only petition in the Lord's Prayer that our Saviour deemed it necessary to pass any comment on. And why? Undoubtedly, because He knew what a tight and almost relentless grip it would have on many hearts in all ages. To cherish ill-feeling and hatred in our hearts is a damning sin; and the sooner men understand it the better for them.

7. "I must become better before I can become a Christian."

The difficulty with this class of inquirers is that they feel that they must attain to a certain degree of moral character before they can be accepted by Jesus Christ. This attitude toward salvation is fundamentally wrong. It seeks to make salvation dependent partly upon works and partly upon grace, whereas salvation is all of grace. A man must come to Christ as a poor lost and helpless sinner with nothing but his sins to plead.

> Nothing in my hand I bring,
> Simply to Thy cross I cling;
> Naked, come to Thee for dress;
> Helpless, look to Thee for grace;
> Foul, I to the fountain fly;
> Wash me, Saviour, or I die.

The following passages are effective in dealing with this class:

Matt. 9:12, 13:

> But when Jesus heard that, he said unto them, They that be whole need not a physician, but they that are sick.
> But go ye and learn what that meaneth, I will have mercy, and not sacrifice: for I am not come to call the righteous, but sinners to repentance.

Rom. 5:6-8:

> For when we were yet without strength, in due time Christ died for the ungodly.
> For scarcely for a righteous man will one die: yet peradventure for a good man some would even dare to die.
> But God commendeth his love toward us, in that, while we were yet sinners, Christ died for us.

In these passages we are taught that Christ came not to save those who were good and righteous, or who had attained a certain degree of morality; indeed, the opposite is the case, he came to save the sinful and the unworthy.

It will be well to use illustrations from the Scriptures which show the willingness of God to save sinners just as they are. The prodigal son (Luke 15:18-24), was received just as he was; the thief on the cross (Luke 23:39-43) surely had no time for reformation, and yet he was received by Christ. The parable of the Pharisee and the Publican (Luke 18:10-14) is a splendid illustration of the truth that a man must take the sinner's place in order to be received.

THE SELF-RIGHTEOUS

CHAPTER VIII.

IV. THE SELF-RIGHTEOUS.

THE people composing this class may be designated as those, who, being approached upon the subject of Christianity, begin at once to minimize the simple, Christ-like faith of the Gospel, and magnify their own good works. They say: "We are honest; we pay our debts; we observe the Golden Rule in all our dealings; we are liberal and beneficent in our gifts to charity, and upon these things we base our hopes for the future welfare of the soul."

Now, the question paramount in this case is this: Can the good works and meritorious deeds of men prove a sufficient basis for the inheriting of life eternal? or do men need the cleansing blood of Jesus Christ to wash away their sins, and the impeccable merits of the Saviour to be put to their account? On what does a man's hope of heaven depend? Upon himself or upon the Christ? To what source shall we look for a definite and conclusive answer to a question so important and fraught with such great and eternal issues? Surely our recourse must be to the Word of the living God.

How shall we proceed to deal with this class of persons? Use such passages of Scripture as will be likely to show them the futility of their mere human merits.

1. **Show them that the Bible teaches salvation by faith in the merits of Christ, and not in the good works of men.**

The following passages will reveal this truth:

Rom. 3:20:

> Therefore by the deeds of the law there shall no flesh
> be justified in his sight; for by the law is the knowl-
> edge of sin.

Rom. 4:2-6:

> For if Abraham were justified by works, he hath
> whereof to glory; but not before God.
> For what saith the Scripture? Abraham believed
> God and it was counted unto him for righteousness.
> Now to him that worketh is the reward not reckoned
> of grace, but of debt.
> But to him that worketh not, but believeth on him
> that justifieth the ungodly, his faith is counted for
> righteousness.
> Even as David also describeth the blessedness of the
> man unto whom God imputeth righteousness without
> works.

Also Gal. 2:16, 3:10, 11.

From these and numerous other passages we are
taught that "good works," which are exceedingly val-
uable as the results and consequence of faith in Christ,
yet have no saving merits whatever, when separated
from that which gives them real value in the currency
of heaven.

**℃. Show them that God looks not only upon the outward acts
of life, but upon the inner, hidden motive of the heart.**

In the eyes of God actions are estimated, not by the
exterior form, but by the inner power and motive which
prompted them.   Many good deeds would lose this
qualifying adjective if measured by the motive which
caused them.   The following passages bring out this
truth very forcefully:

Luke 16:15:

> And he [Jesus] said unto them, Ye are they which
> justify yourselves before men; but God knoweth your
> hearts; for that which is highly esteemed among men
> is abomination in the sight of God.

Prov. 16:2:

> All the ways of a man are clean in his own eyes; but the Lord weigheth the spirits.

Isa. 64:6:

> But we are all as an unclean thing, and all our righteousnesses are as filthy rags.

Also Jer. 17:9, 10; Phil. 3:9; 1 Sam. 16:7; Prov. 30:12.

One important thought is borne home upon us as we read these passages, and it is this: the absolute worthlessness of all action not based on right motives. Let us, as Christian workers, seek to impress those with whom we deal with this solemn truth.

3. Show that we can please God by faith only.

The Jews asked Jesus in John 6:28, 29:

> What shall we do, that we might work the works of God?

Jesus replied:

> This is the work of God, that ye believe on him whom he hath sent.

Faith alone gives us the right to draw near to God at all:

Heb. 11:6:

> But without faith it is impossible to please him [God].

These verses contain in simple formula the complete solution of the relation of works and faith.

4. Show them from the Scriptures that such a belief in the meritorious significance of good works makes void, ignores, neutralizes, the death of Christ as the ground of our salvation.

This truth is contained in such passages as Gal. 2:21:

I do not frustrate [or make void] the grace of God: for if righteousness come by the law, then Christ is dead in vain [or for naught].

5. **Give illustrations from the Scriptures of good, moral men, who nevertheless needed a change of heart, who needed saving faith in Jesus Christ, as a fitness for inheritance in the kingdom of God.**

Cornelius (Acts 10:1-6 and 11:11-14) and Paul (Phil. 3:4-8) furnish very striking illustrations of the necessity of something more than mere human goodness and morality to fit a man for entrance into the kingdom of heaven. Jesus' own words are very emphatic in this connection: "Except a man may be born again [or from above], he cannot see the kingdom of God."

THE BACKSLIDER

CHAPTER IX.

V. THE BACKSLIDER.

THE backslider is at once the easiest and yet the hardest case to deal with, according as he is penitent or impenitent.

By the backslider is meant the one who, having begun the Christian life, has given it up for one reason or another; the one who, having put his hand to the plough, has turned back.

"Backslider" is not a New Testament word, and occurs but once in the Old Testament (Prov. 14:14).

How To Deal With Them.

1. **Remember that all professing backsliders are not so in reality. Some backsliders have never really slid forward. The following passages clearly show this:**

1 John 2:19:

> They went out from us, but they were not of us; for if they had been of us, they would no doubt have continued with us; but they went out, that they might be made manifest that they were not all of us.

2 Pet. 2:20-22:

> For if, after they have escaped the pollutions of the world through the knowledge of the Lord and Saviour Jesus Christ, they are again entangled therein, and overcome, the latter end is worse with them than the beginning.
>
> For it had been better for them not to have known the way of righteousness, than, after they have known it, to turn from the holy commandment delivered unto them.
>
> But it is happened unto them according to the true proverb, The dog is turned to his own vomit again; and the sow that was washed to her wallowing in the mire.

Compare also Matt. 13:20, 21; Mark 4:16, 17; Heb. 10:38, 39.

Many, like Jesus, tasted, but did not drink (Matt. 27:34).

It may not be so easy as we think for the righteous man to go out of his way to backslide.

Job 17:9:

> The righteous also shall hold on his way, and he that hath clean hands shall be stronger and stronger.

2. Seek to ascertain the cause of the backsliding.

This is important, because the very thing which led the inquirer to backslide may be the very thing which is keeping him from coming back. All such obstacles must be removed. Some of the causes of backsliding are as follows:

(a) Mis-treatment by, or inconsistencies of Christians.

Meet this difficulty with

Jer. 2:5:

> Thus saith the Lord, What iniquity have your fathers found in me, that they are gone far from me, and have walked after vanity, and are become vain?

Isa. 5:4:

> What could have been done more to my vineyard, that I have not done in it? wherefore, when I looked that it should bring forth grapes, brought it forth wild grapes?

Ask what wrong God has done to them? Why should they treat God so?

(b) It may be the indulgence of known sin, or the neglect of the means of grace, or some worldly alliance that is the cause of the backslidden condition.

Be sure to find out the cause. Unless you do, you cannot deal with the case effectually.

In your dealing with backsliders, you will find they fall into two classes: the penitent and the impenitent

The Penitent Backslider.

By this term we mean the backslider who is sorry for his sin, and desires to return, even though he may feel that he may not be received.

1. Show God's willingness to receive all who come back to Him.

Luke 15:11-24—The parable of the Prodigal Son. Probably no other part of the Scriptures is so applicable and so winning as this parable. Use also:

Jer. 3:12, 13:

> Go and proclaim these words toward the north, and say, Return, thou backsliding Israel, saith the Lord; and I will not cause mine anger to fall upon you: for I am merciful, saith the Lord, and I will not keep anger forever.
>
> Only acknowledge thine iniquity, that thou hast transgressed against the Lord thy God, and hast scattered thy ways to the strangers under every green tree, and ye have not obeyed my voice, saith the Lord.

Mark 16:7:

> But go your way, tell his disciples and Peter that he goeth before you into Galilee: there shall ye see him, as he said unto you.

Recount the story of Peter's denial, then show by this passage how Christ sent a special message of forgiveness to him.

2. Show what God demands in order to effect restoration.

2 Chron. 7:14:

> If my people, which are called by my name, shall humble themselves, and pray, and seek my face, and turn from their wicked ways; then will I hear from heaven, and will forgive their sin, and will heal their land.

1 John 1:9:

> If we confess our sins, he is faithful and just to forgive us our sins, and to cleanse us from all unrighteousness.

Also Jer. 3:12-14; Hosea 14:1, 2, 4.

These passages show the inquirer how to come back to God. Obeyed, they bring back the sense and consciousness of a right relationship with God.

3. It will be well to give instructions as to how to grow in grace, and not backslide again. See page 107.

THE IMPENITENT BACKSLIDER.

Sometimes backsliders are indifferent and obstinate, and must be dealt with accordingly. This class does not manifest any sorrow for their backsliding; neither do they exhibit any desire to return to the Lord from whom they have wandered. Possibly the best method of dealing with such inquirers is to show them the awful sin they have committed in not continuing to follow the Lord, and what are the awful, fatal, and inevitable consequences now, and, most of all, in the world to come.

The following references reveal these heart-searching truths:

Jer. 2:13, 19:

> For my people have committed two evils; they have forsaken me the fountain of living waters, and hewed them out cisterns, broken cisterns, that can hold no water.
> Thine own wickedness shall correct thee, and thy backslidings shall reprove thee; know therefore and see that it is an evil thing and bitter, that thou hast forsaken the Lord thy God, and that my fear is not in thee, saith the Lord God of hosts.

1 Kings 11:9:

> And the Lord was angry with Solomon, because his heart was turned from the Lord God of Israel, which had appeared unto him twice.

Amos 4:11:

> I have overthrown some of you, as God overthrew Sodom and Gomorrah, and ye were as a firebrand plucked out of the burning: yet have ye not returned unto me, saith the Lord.

Also 2 Peter 2:20-22; Luke 11:24, 26

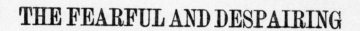

THE FEARFUL AND DESPAIRING

CHAPTER X.

VI. THE FEARFUL AND DESPAIRING.

1. "I am afraid I will be persecuted if I become a Christian."

THIS objection is more general than we might, on first thought, think. There are, doubtless, many people who now are not Christians, who would speedily become such if only they thought they were strong enough to brave the laugh, the sneer, and the rebuff of their worldly companions. Again, this objection has great weight in deciding the question of a man's ability to courageously face ridicule, which, in itself, is a greater test of heroism than the feat of a Hobson or a Funston. Many a man who has never hesitated to take the front rank and face the cannon's mouth in the day of battle, has failed ignominiously when the opportunity to witness for Christ has presented itself to him in the line of his everyday duty.

We must not, therefore, treat this excuse lightly. On the contrary, we must endeavor to point the inquirer to Him who giveth strength to them that are weak and fearful.

The best method to pursue in this case is to use such passages of Scripture as show the folly of the "fear of man" and the blessedness, both here and hereafter, for those who boldly confess Him before the world.

This objection may be summed up under four divisions:

(a) Those who are afraid of the ridicule of their companions.

Show them that they are not to be afraid of the ridicule of man; they must seek to covet the approval of God. Only fatal consequences can result from the fear of man.

Prov. 29:25:

> The fear of man bringeth a snare; but whoso putteth his trust in the Lord shall be safe.

This passage shows that the fear of man involves men in danger and misfortune. The word "fear" in this verse means the regulation of one's conduct by the opinion of morally untrained men. To thus regulate one's life is to fall into a snare which involves the loss of the soul. (Also use Prov. 13:20.)

Luke 12:4, 5:

> And I say unto you my friends, Be not afraid of them that kill the body, and after that have no more that they can do.
> But I will forewarn you whom ye shall fear: Fear him, which after he hath killed hath power to cast into hell; yea, I say unto you, Fear him.

Here we are shown whom we should fear. We should fear God, who has the greatest power.

Use also Isa. 51:7, 8, 12; Jer. 1:8, 17: Mark 8:38.

(b) Those who are afraid they will lose their friends if they become Christians.

Ofttimes men do lose friends when they become Christians. Without doubt this fear keeps many from accepting Christ. How shall we deal with them? In the following way:

(1) Show the inquirer that such friends are not worthy of his company, for they are enemies of God.

Any man who does not wish a Christian success is thereby constituted an enemy of God. This is distinctly taught in James 4:4:

> Ye adulterers and adulteresses, know ye not that the friendship of the world is enmity with God? whosoever therefore will be a friend of the world is the enemy of God.

(2) Show him that he gains a more worthy companionship (Mark 10:29, 30).

In the first place, he gains the companionship of Christ, and then the companionship of Christian people. The inquirer, therefore, is called upon to make a choice of his company. Who would not be willing to give up an earthly friend for a heavenly Friend—to surrender the human for the divine, the temporal for the eternal?

(3) Show him that a special blessing is pronounced upon those who choose the righteous as their companions.

Psa. 1:1, 2:

> Blessed is the man that walketh not in the counsel of the ungodly, nor standeth in the way of sinners, nor sitteth in the seat of the scornful.
> But his delight is in the law of the Lord; and in his law doth he meditate day and night.

(c) "I will be persecuted by my friends if I become a Christian."

Do not deny this statement, for it is true.

(1) Show the inquirer that this is what is to be expected.

2 Tim. 3:12:

> Yea, and all that will live godly in Christ Jesus shall suffer persecution.

This passage teaches that everyone bent on living godly in this world is bound to suffer persecution. On the other hand, the inquirer may be shown:

(2) That it is a great honor and privilege to suffer for Christ.

Acts 5:40, 41:

> And to him they agreed: and when they had called the apostles and beaten them, they commanded that

> they should not speak in the name of Jesus, and let
> them go.
> And they departed from the presence of the council,
> rejoicing that they were counted worthy to suffer shame
> for his name.

Also 1 Pet. 2 :20, 21.

(3) The result of suffering with Christ.

Matt. 5 :10-12 :

> Blessed are they which are persecuted for righteous-
> ness' sake : for theirs is the kingdom of heaven.
> Blessed are ye, when men shall revile you, and per-
> secute you, and shall say all manner of evil against
> you falsely, for my sake.
> Rejoice, and be exceeding glad : for great is your re-
> ward in heaven : for so persecuted they the prophets
> which were before you.

When men revile us and abuse us, we should exult
and leap for joy.

(4) Show the future reward.

2 Tim. 2 :12 :

> If we suffer, we shall also reign with him : if we deny
> him he also will deny us.

*(d) Show the inquirer the possibility of his being
able to influence his companions for Christ.*

This is a phase of the subject which is often overlooked.

**2. "I am afraid that if I start to be a Christian, I shall be
unable to keep it up; I am so weak."**

The way to deal with this class of inquirers is to
use such passages of Scripture as shall set forth the
fact that the God whom we serve is able to deliver
us in every hour of temptation; that our "standing in
grace" does not depend upon our strength, but upon
God's: that it is the will of Christ that we should be
more than conquerors over the world, the flesh, and
the devil.

Jude 24:

> Now unto him that is able to keep you from falling, and to present you faultless before the presence of his glory with exceeding joy.

This passage gives us the assurance that God is able to keep us from "stumbling." (R. V.) We do not keep ourselves; God is our keeper.

1 Cor. 10:13:

> There hath no temptation taken you but such as is common to man: but God is faithful, who will not suffer you to be tempted above that ye are able; but will with the temptation also make a way to escape, that ye may be able to bear it.

What a grand promise this is! God assures us that we shall never be tempted above what we are able, through His grace, to bear; that a way of escape will always be planned for us by Him.

> The cross that He gave may be heavy,
> But it ne'er outweighs His grace;
> The storm that I feared may surround me,
> But it ne'er excludes His face.

With such a glorious promise as this who would fear to venture on Christ?

Phil. 1:6:

> Being confident of this very thing, that he which hath begun a good work in you will perform it until the day of Jesus Christ.

What a confidence! God will never leave the work He has begun in any soul unfinished. He who begins the work completes it also. A finished, completed redemption is the possible possession of the humblest soul that commits itself to the great Father in heaven.

Isa. 41:10, 13, 14:

> Fear thou not; for I am with thee; be not dismayed; for I am thy God; I will strengthen thee; yea, I will help thee; yea, I will uphold thee with the right hand of my righteousness.

> For I the Lord thy God will hold thy right hand, say-
> ing unto thee, Fear not; I will help thee.
> Fear not, thou worm Jacob, and ye men of Israel; I
> will help thee, saith the Lord, and thy redeemer, the
> Holy One of Israel.

Note here that God takes hold of our right hand with
His right hand. Who is able to pluck us out of His
great, strong, mighty, omnipotent hand? Not man,
nor angel, nor devil. Why, then, are we fearful as to
what the issues of our trusting in Him will be?

2 Tim. 1:12:

> Nevertheless I am not ashamed: for I know whom I
> have believed, and am persuaded that he is able to keep
> that which I have committed unto him against that day.

This verse is the Christian's safety deposit vault.
When the soul commits itself to the Lord Jesus Christ
for safe keeping, there is no fear but that He will
guard it safely. It is a safe investment.

The following passages also can be used to great
advantage:

2 Cor. 12:9, 10; John 17:12; Deut. 33:27; John 10:
27-29.

What great passages of Scripture these are! Who
can measure the length, the breadth, the depth, the
height of their meaning? And yet all their fullness of
meaning is for the encouragement of the timid, weak,
and fearful disciple.

> What have I to fear, with my Lord so near,
> Leaning on the 'Everlasting Arms'?

3. **"I am afraid Jesus will not receive me."**

One of the objections frequently urged against becoming a Christian is the above. I have always found
the following a very good verse to use with this class:

John 6:37:

> All that the Father giveth me shall come to me; and
> him that cometh to me I will in no wise cast out.

Use it like this: "Who is it that Jesus will not cast
out?" "Him that cometh." "And if you come, what
does Jesus say He will do?" "Receive me." "Well,
then, all you have to do is to believe His Word and
come to Him."

Use also:

Rev. 22:17:

> And the Spirit and the bride say, Come. And let
> him that heareth say, Come. And let him that is
> athirst come. And whosoever will, let him take the
> water of life freely.

Rom. 10:13:

> For whosoever shall call upon the name of the Lord
> shall be saved.

John 3:16:

> For God so loved the world, that he gave his only
> begotten Son, that whosoever believeth in him should not
> perish, but have everlasting life.

Ask: "Whom does 'whosoever' mean?" If the word
means anything at all, it means "anyone." So anyone
may come.

By using the narratives of the Sinful Woman (Luke
7:37-50), and the Prodigal Son (Luke 15:11-32), you
can illustrate God's willingness to receive sinners. In
the following—

Luke 15:2:

> And the Pharisees and scribes murmured, saying,
> This man receiveth sinners, and eateth with them.

we have the definite and explicit statement that, "this
man [Jesus] receiveth sinners." Although this was
the statement of the enemies of Christ, it is nevertheless
true of Him, probably doubly so because of this fact.

4. "I have tried before and failed."

We need to have a great deal of patience in dealing with this class. It is very much harder to try to live a Christian life after one has tried and failed than to try for the first time. The Christian worker must by no means overlook this fact. Deal with this class in the following wa

(a) Assert the possibility of success.

To do this, use 2 Cor. 9:8, 10:

> And God is able to make all grace abound toward you: that ye, always having all sufficiency in all things, may abound to every good work:
> Now he that ministereth seed to the sower both minister bread for your food, and multiply your seed sown, and increase the fruits of your righteousness:

Verse 8 shows that God has the power to enable us to make a success of the Christian life, and, therefore, shows its possibility. Verse 10 shows us that God will do it, and, therefore, asserts its reality.

(b) Ascertain the cause of failure.

Many professing Christians have failed in the Christian life simply because they have not lived it, or they did not start right. Ask the following questions:

(1) Did you absolutely trust in Christ and in His finished work for your salvation? Did you depend upon faith or upon feeling? Did you get a clear vision of Christ as your sin-bearer? (Isa. 53:6.)

(2) Did you absolutely surrender yourself to Christ? or did you keep back something?—did you retain any idol in your heart? Anything less than a full surrender means failure.

(3) Did you confess Christ publicly? To be ashamed of Christ is a stepping-stone to failure. An open confession lets men know where you stand. Many a man has failed in the Christian life because he has failed to let people know where he stood.

(4) Did you pray constantly? Prayer is to the soul what breathing is to the body—it is the Christian's vital breath.

(5) Did you study the Bible daily? Here is the fundamental cause of failure. There must be a daily study of the Bible if there is to be growth in grace (Acts 17:11; 1 Pet. 2:2).

(6) Did you go to work for Christ? Rust is the witness of failure; idleness is the devil's workshop. The probabilities are that, unless we seek to lead others to Christ, we will lose our grip on Christ ourselves.

It may be found from the above questions that the inquirer has tried to live *a* Christian life, but not *the* Christian life.

(c) Give instructions as to how to make a success of the Christian life.

It is much better to lead one soul into a place of success in the Christian life than to deal with half a dozen in an inadequate manner. We must realize the danger of backsliding. Satan is active in every man's life, more so after a man's conversion than before. The following scriptures will be helpful in pointing the way of success:

(1) Make a full surrender (Rom. 12:1, 14, 20-22).

(2) Prayer (Luke 18:1; Matt. 26:41).

(3) Constant reading of the Bible (Acts 17:11; 20:32; 1 Pet. 2:2).

(4) Faithfulness to the church and its ordinances (Heb. 10:25; Acts 2:41-47).

(5) Go to work for Christ (John 1:41-45; Matt. 20:1-16).

5. "I have sinned away the day of grace."

Just what the inquirer means by this statement is not always clear. This the worker must find out. Whatever may be meant by it, a sad spiritual condition is thereby indicated, and very tender and delicate treatment is needed.

(a) Find out what he means by the statement.

Usually the inquirer means that he has gone by "Past Redemption Point"; sinned so grievously, willfully, persistently against light and knowledge that there is no further hope for him.

These statements are usually made because of his misunderstanding of some passages of Scripture—the following, for example:

Gen. 6:3:

> My Spirit shall not always strive with man.

He infers from this passage that there is a time when the Spirit of God ceases to strive with a man, and leaves him to his doom. This is a false interpretation, for this verse deals with the race and not with an individual; again, it deals with the continuation, and not with the cutting off—"his days shall be a hundred and twenty years"—of the probation period of the human race; indeed, the length of the life of the individual is not in the question here; and, further, the verse indicates that nothing but the cessation of the human race would put an end to the striving of the Spirit.

Heb. 6:4-6:

> For it is impossible for those who were once enlightened, and have tasted of the heavenly gift, and were made partakers of the Holy Ghost,
> And have tasted the good word of God, and the powers of the world to come,
> If they shall fall away, to renew them again unto repentance; seeing they crucify to themselves the Son of God afresh, and put him to an open shame.

Heb. 10:26:

> For if we sin willfully after that we have received the knowledge of the truth, there remaineth no more sacrifice for sins.

These scriptures also are used to buttress the cause of the despairing. A careful reading of these passages in the Revised Version would remove this erroneous interpretation. The first of these two scriptures teaches that it is "impossible to renew" those described in these verses, not under *any* condition, but only *"the while they are crucifying the Son of God afresh,"* etc. How can you save any man who is deliberately turning his back on the cross of Christ? The latter passage (10:26) does not teach that a man who was once a Christian and has sinned willfully since he became such has no further hope of forgiveness. It teaches that, if a man who has once seen in the cross of Christ his only hope of salvation, deliberately turns away from that cross, then there is *"no other,"* or "any more a [or another] sacrifice for sin."

In dealing with this class be very slow to believe that such a condition as being beyond hope, actually exists—at least in a soul that is at all concerned about the matter.

(b) Such passages as the following may be used to show that all are welcome to come to Christ.

John 6:37:

> All that the Father giveth me shall come to me; and him that cometh to me I will in no wise cast out.

Rev. 22:17:

> And the Spirit and the bride say, Come. And let him that heareth say, Come. And let him that is athirst come. And whosoever will, let him take the water of life freely.

Also Rom. 10:13.

If the inquirer points to Heb. 12:17:

> For ye know how that afterward, when he would have
> inherited the blessing, he was rejected: for he found no
> place of repentance, though he sought it carefully
> with tears.

as indicating the possibility of there being a time when
a man cannot repent, you may draw his attention to
the fact that this verse has nothing to say with reference to a man's relation to God; it speaks only of
Esau's inability to change the mind of his father with
reference to the stolen blessing.

**6. "I have committed the unpardonable sin—the sin against
the Holy Ghost."**

This excuse is based upon the following passages:

Matt. 12:30-32:

> He that is not with me is against me; and he that
> gathereth not with me scattereth abroad.
> Wherefore I say unto you, All manner of sin and
> blasphemy shall be forgiven unto men: but the blas-
> phemy against the Holy Ghost shall not be forgiven
> unto men.
> And whosoever speaketh a word against the Son of
> man, it shall be forgiven him: but whosoever speaketh
> against the Holy Ghost, it shall not be forgiven him,
> neither in this world, neither in the world to come.

Compare Mark 3:28-30:

1 John 5:16:

> If any man see his brother sin a sin which is not
> unto death, he shall ask, and he shall give him life for
> them that sin not unto death. There is a sin unto death:
> I do not say that he shall pray for it.

*(a) Try to find out from the inquirer what he means
by the sin against the Holy Ghost.*

You will find that in almost every case he will not be
able to define it. It might seem therefore as though
it were not necessary to deal with a sin that is not
definable. And possibly that is right. It is much
better to get the inquirer's mind away from the sin he

thinks he has committed and fix it on those passages
of Scripture which hold out forgiveness for "all manner of sin and blasphemy."

1 Tim. 1 :15, 16, with 1 :13 :

> This is a faithful saying, and worthy of all accept-
> ation, that Christ Jesus came into the world to save
> sinners; of whom I am chief.
> Howbeit for this cause I obtained mercy, that in me
> first Jesus Christ might show forth all longsuffering,
> for a pattern to them which should hereafter believe on
> him to life everlasting.
> Who was before a blasphemer, and a persecutor, and
> injurious: but I obtained mercy, because I did it igno-
> rantly in unbelief.

These verses show that, although Paul was a blas-
phemer, he nevertheless obtained forgiveness. Further,
his forgiveness is an encouragement to all others, who,
having seen the awfulness of the sin of blasphemy, desire to repent.

1 John 5 :16 (above) does not speak of a *specific* sin
for which there is no forgiveness. The Revised Version
leaves out the word "a," and translates the verse,
"There is sin unto death." This might seem to imply
that this sin is a state rather than an act.

*(b) Use the following scriptures to show the willing-
ness of Christ to receive and forgive all those who come
to Him.*

John 6 :37; Rev. 22 :17; Acts 13 :38, 39; Rom. 10 :13.

(For full quotation of these passages see under 5, *b*.)

7. "It is too late now for me to become a Christian."

This excuse is based on a wrong interpretation of
Proverbs 1 :24-31. Emphasize the fact that those who
call, in these verses, are calling from wrong motives.
Show them from the following passages that it is not
too late; that, on the contrary, it is the proper time.

2 Cor. 6 :2 :

> For he saith, I have heard thee in a time accepted, and in the day of salvation have I succoured thee; behold, now is the accepted time; behold, now is the day of salvation.

Heb. 4 :7 :

> Again, he limiteth a certain day, saying in David, To-day, after so long a time; as it is said, To-day if ye will hear his voice, harden not your hearts.

Also Deut. 4 :29-31.

THE PROCRASTINATOR

CHAPTER XI.

VII. THE PROCRASTINATOR.

THOSE who desire to put off their salvation until another time form a very numerous class, and one very difficult to deal with. There is, seemingly, to the one offering it, less guilt connected with this excuse than, for example, with one that borders on the nature of unbelief. For this reason many people put off their salvation until it is too late. Either they are cut off suddenly or they are so racked with pain or lulled by drugs that the time they had set aside for settling the affairs of the soul does not come in a propitious way. It is with them as it was with Nebuchadnezzar's image: the lower the members, the coarser the metal; the farther off the time, the more unfit. "Today is the golden opportunity; tomorrow will be the silver season; next day but the brazen one; and so on, till at last I shall come to the toes of clay, and be turned to dust." The *Biblical Treasury* furnishes the following story:

"A minister of the Gospel determined on one occasion to preach on the text, 'Now is the accepted time; now is the day of salvation.' Whilst in his study thinking, he fell asleep, and dreamed that he was carried into hell, and set down in the midst of a conclave of lost spirits. They were assembled to devise means whereby they might get at the souls of men. One rose and said, 'I will go to the earth and tell men that the Bible is all a fable, that it is not divinely appointed of God.' No, that would not do. Another said, 'Let me go. I will tell men that there is no God, no Saviour, no heaven, no hell'; and at the last words a fiendish smile lighted upon all their countenances. 'No, that will not do; we cannot make men believe *that.*' Suddenly one arose, and with a wise mien, like the serpent of old, suggested, 'No, I will journey to the world of men, and tell them that there *is* a God, that there *is* a Saviour, that there *is* a heaven,—yes, and a hell, too,—but I will tell them *there is no hurry; tomorrow will do;* it will be even as today.' And they sent him."

This excuse assumes different forms of Expression:

1. "I want to get established in business first: after that I will be a Christian."

The following passages are good to use with this class:

Matt. 6:33:

> But seek ye first the kingdom of God, and his righteousness; and all these things shall be added unto you.

Show from this verse that the first business of every man is to settle his interests with reference to his relation to the kingdom of God.

Also Luke 12:16-21—The Rich Fool.

This parable shows the utter folly as well as the awful doom of those who seek to be established in business before religion. What did his being established in business profit him? He "gained the world," but "lost his soul." Apply this story to the case you have in hand something like this: "Suppose you do get established in business, what assurance have you, more than this rich fool had, that you will have the time, or even the desire to turn to God and seek for salvation?"

James 4:13-17:

> Go to now, ye that say, Today or tomorrow we will go into such a city, and continue there a year, and buy and sell, and get gain:

Whereas ye know not what shall be on the morrow. For what is your life? It is even a vapour, that appeareth for a little time, and then vanisheth away.

For that ye ought to say, If the Lord will, we shall live, and do this, or that.

But now ye rejoice in your boastings: all such rejoicing is evil.

Therefore to him that knoweth to do good, and doeth it not, to him it is sin.

Show from this that a man may be cut off right in the midst of his seeking to establish himself in business; that a really thoughtful man ought to look after the interests of his soul at once, inasmuch as he "knows not what shall be on the morrow." God should be put *first*—"if God will," etc.; not *last*, as in the case of the rich fool.

2. "I will wait until I get older, then I will become a Christian."

Use Eccl. 12:1, 2 with 2 Sam. 19:35, and Heb. 3:13 (given in order below):

Remember now thy Creator in the days of thy youth, while the evil days come not, nor the years draw nigh, when thou shalt say, I have no pleasure in them;

While the sun, or the light, or the moon, or the stars, be not darkened, nor the clouds return after the rain.

I am this day fourscore years old; and can I discern between good and evil? can thy servant taste what I eat or what I drink? can I hear any more the voice of singing men and singing women? wherefore then should thy servant be yet a burden unto my lord the king?

But exhort one another daily, while it is called Today; lest any of you be hardened through the deceitfulness of sin.

These verses show clearly that the longer one waits before giving his heart to God, the harder his heart becomes, and the more difficult it is for him to become a Christian. The young and tender years are the years wherein one should seek to know the Lord. The worker may endeavor to show the contemptibleness of throwing away the best years of one's life in the service of Satan and sin, and then offering the very end of it, the which, probably, is of no use to him or anybody else, to God. If he will not give himself to God in

"the green tree," the odds are against his doing it "in
the dry." Why have a life wasted and a soul saved,
when you can have both life and soul saved and useful
in the service of the kingdom of God?

3. "I am determined to become a Christian before I die."

Show from the following passages that this position
is a false one, and for these reasons:

No man knows when he is going to die; no man
"knoweth the day of his death."

Prov. 29:1:

> He, that being often reproved hardeneth his neck, shall
> suddenly be destroyed, and that without remedy.

Also Job 34:20, and Luke 12:20; James 4:13-17.

He may die "suddenly," "in a moment," "this night."
Who knows? What utter folly, therefore, to put off
so important a matter until so uncertain a date.
Draw the attention to the sudden deaths occurring
around him daily. Ask him if he does not recall such
within his own knowledge?

Again, this position is a false one because it assumes
that a man will surely call, or feel like calling upon
God in the last hours of his life, which, of course, is
by no means the case. This may be proved by referring
to the story of the impenitent thief (Luke 23:39), who
used his last breath to rail upon Jesus Christ. It is
all very well for people to draw our attention to the
fact that the dying thief was saved in the last hour;
they seem to forget that the other dying thief was lost
in the last hour. The probabilities are that we will
die as we have lived. Deathbed repentances are by no
means to be depended upon. Every pastor will bear
testimony to the truth of this statement. Repentances
during the last hours of life are prompted by fear very
largely—a fear shown to be anything but the right

kind of fear, and soon forgotten in case the sick person is raised up from what seemed for a time to be his deathbed. In these days of anæsthetics it is almost impossible for one to die in possession of his full senses. How then can a man attend to the matters of the soul which require thoughtful attention? And then, sudden death may overtake us, and thus we may be robbed of a deathbed upon which to repent.

Use the following passages, and question the inquirer on the truth contained in them touching his particular case:

Isa. 55:6:

> Seek ye the Lord while he may be found, call ye upon him while he is near.

Luke 13:24, 25:

> Strive to enter in at the strait gate; for many, I say unto you, will seek to enter in, and shall not be able.
> When once the master of the house is risen up, and hath shut to the door, and ye begin to stand without, and to knock at the door, saying, Lord, Lord, open unto us; and he shall answer and say unto you, I know you not whence ye are.

Use also, if necessary, Prov. 1:28 (context, vs. 24-31); 2 Cor. 6:2; Prov. 27:1; Heb. 4:7; 12:17.

> There is a time, we know not when,
>   A place, we know not where;
> Which marks the destiny of men
>   To glory or despair.
>
> There is a line, by us unseen,
>   Which crosses every path,
> Which marks the boundary between
>   God's mercy and his wrath.
>
> To pass that limit is to die,
>   To die as if by stealth;
> It does not dim the beaming eye,
>   Nor pale the glow of health.
>
> The conscience may be still at ease,
>   The spirit light and gay;
> And that which pleases still may please,
>   And care be thrust away.

But on that forehead God hath set
  Indelibly a mark;
Unseen by man, for man as yet,
  Is blind and in the dark.

He feels perchance that all is well
  And every fear is calmed;
He lives, he dies, he wakes in hell,
  Not only doomed, but damned!

O, where is that mysterious line
  That may by men be crossed,
Beyond which God himself hath sworn,
  That he who goes is lost?

An answer from the skies repeats,
  "Ye who from God depart,"
TODAY, O hear His voice,
  TODAY repent and harden not your heart.
                    —Joseph Addison Alexander.

THE FAULT-FINDING

CHAPTER XII.

VIII. THE FAULT-FINDING.

EVER since the days when the Apostle Paul cried out, "Is God unrighteous?" or "Is there unrighteousness with God?" have some of the sons of men been answering affirmatively the question which the apostle answered negatively. "God is not unrighteous," and men must be made to understand this. We must not, as Job's friends did, attribute folly to God. We must say to Him, "Arise, O God, plead Thine own cause: remember how foolish man reproacheth Thee daily." Yet, it is true, that these gainsayers, these men "who speak evil of the things they understand not," must be dealt with and reproved by the Christian worker. God beseeches men through us.

This general class of objectors states its case in varied aspects, viz.:

THOSE WHO FIND FAULT WITH GOD.

1. "It is unjust of God to create men and then condemn them."

What shall we say to this charge against God? and how shall we answer it? "To the law and to the testimony," we must resort for our weapons, for this warfare is not carnal but spiritual. We must take "the sword of the Spirit, which is the Word of God."

(a) Use such passages as show God's purpose in creation.

Isa. 43:7:

> Even every one that is called by my name: for I have
> created him for my glory, I have formed him; yea, I
> have made him.

Also Rev. 4:11; Psa. 102:18, and Isa. 65:18.

It is very clearly stated in these passages that God
did not create man in order to damn him, but, on the
contrary, that he might live to be a perpetual praise
and find unending glory and blessing in the presence
of God. Everlasting joy and bliss, therefore. char-
acterize the creative purposes of God for man.

*(b) Show from the Scriptures that all God's deal-
ings with man point to His declared intention and desire that man should be saved, not lost.*

Ezek. 33:11:

> Say unto them, As I live, saith the Lord God, I have
> no pleasure in the death of the wicked; but that the
> wicked turn from his way and live: turn ye, turn ye
> from your evil ways; for why will ye die, O house of
> Israel?

John 3:16, 17; 2 Pet. 3:9, and also Matt. 23:37.

Can God's attitude of loving solicitude for man's
eternal salvation be more clearly and earnestly declared than in these words? Does it look as though
God wanted to damn or to save men? Consider the
price the Father paid, the sufferings the Son endured,
that man might be saved from eternal despair, and then
understand how awfully wicked it is to charge God
with such injustice.

*(c) Show them that, if they are eternally lost, it is
because of their wilful rejection of God's way of life
as revealed in the work of Christ.*

Matt. 23:37:

> O Jerusalem, Jerusalem, thou that killest the prophets,
> and stonest them which are sent unto thee, how often
> would I have gathered thy children together, even as a

hen gathereth her chickens under her wings, and ye
would not!

Also John 5:40; 2 Thess. 2:12, and Matt. 25:41.

We learn from these passages that, if men are lost,
it is because they deliberately choose to be lost, know-
ingly and willfully rejecting their only hope of salvation in the redemption of Jesus Christ. Just as the
rich man tumbled into hell, kicking the poor body of
Lazarus which had been laid at his gate to keep him
from such a doom, so the man who has the misfortune
to awake and find himself among the lost in the other
world will realize that he finds himself in hell because
he deliberately stumbled over the crucified body of
Jesus Christ, placed, as it were, at the very mouth of
hell, to keep him out of such a place of torment. It
is not God's creative purpose, but sinful man's perver-
sion, that is the cause of his condemnation.

2. "God has not clearly revealed Himself to man."

There are some people who say, "Why has not God
clearly revealed Himself to man so that he may know
who and what God is, and what He expects of His
creatures? An earthly father would not punish his
child for not doing his will when he had not had that
will made known to him, nor should God." Nor does
He. God never asks the impossible from His children.
He asks obedience up to the light they possess.

*(a) Show the objector that God has revealed Him-
self and His will to men.*

Rom. 1:18-20:

For the wrath of God is revealed from heaven against
all ungodliness and unrighteousness of men, who hold
the truth in unrighteousness;
Because that which may be known of God is manifest
in them; for God hath shewed it unto them.
For the invisible things of him from the creation of
the world are clearly seen, being understood by the
things that are made, even his eternal power and Godhead: so that they are without excuse.

Also 1 Cor. 2:12 and John 1:9.

(b) God has revealed Himself to man in Christ.

John 1:18:

> No man hath seen God at any time; the only begotten Son, which is in the bosom of the Father, he hath declared him.

Also Matt. 11:27; 2 Cor. 5:19, and John 14:9.

(c) Show that sin and disobedience keep man in ignorance of God.

2 Cor. 4:3, 4:

> But if our gospel be hid, it is hid to them that are lost: In whom the god of this world hath blinded the minds of them which believe not, lest the light of the glorious gospel of Christ, who is the image of God, should shine unto them.

Also Rom. 1:21, John 7:17, and Isa. 59:1, 2.

After all, our ignorance of God is due to our unlikeness to Him. Our sins have hid His face from us. Not only is it true that ignorance is sin, but it is also true that sin is ignorance.

(d) Show that willingness to obey the will of God will bring further revelation.

John 7:17:

> If any man will do his will, he shall know of the doctrine, whether it be of God, or whether I speak of myself.

Also Hosea 6:3.

THOSE WHO FIND FAULT WITH THE BIBLE.

Objection to the Word of God finds its expression in various ways:

1. "The Bible is foolishness."

In dealing with this class of objectors it is a good thing to say: "You are right, my friend, for that is

just what the Bible itself says." Then you may find
1 Cor. 1:18, 23, 24:

> For the preaching of the cross is to them that perish
> foolishness; but unto us which are saved it is the power
> of God.
> But we preach Christ crucified, unto the Jews a stum-
> blingblock, and unto the Greeks foolishness.
> But unto them which are called, both Jews and Greeks,
> Christ the power of God, and the wisdom of God.

Get him to read these verses for himself. Ask him,
"To whom is the Bible and the preaching of the cross
foolishness?" To those who are perishing in sin. To
the one who receives it, it is "the power of God and
the wisdom of God."

Show him further, 1 Cor. 2:14.

Here it is the "natural," *i. e.*, the soulish, fleshly,
worldly, sinning man to whom the Bible is foolishness;
the fault is not with the Bible, but with the man's sin.

By the use of Isa. 5:24, show him the penalty of thus
rejecting the Word of the Lord.

2. "The Bible is full of contradictions."

Ask him to show you one. You will find that the
man who growls most about the contradictions in the
Bible is not able to show you one. A Christian worker,
in an inquiry room, was addressed thus by one of these
blatant infidels: "Don't talk to me about your religion
and your Bible, for I don't believe them. That Bible
you have in your hand is full of contradictions; why
should I then believe it?" The worker feigned sur-
prise and timidity, and said: "Well, that is news to
me; I am not aware that there are any contradictions
in the Bible." "Yes, there are," said the infidel, wax-
ing bold at the timidity of the worker and the increas-
ing interest of the onlookers, "I could show you scores
of them; the Bible is full of them." This was just the
point the worker desired to bring the infidel to in order
to justly humiliate him. "Then," said the worker, with

the suddenness and force of an avalanche, "you can surely show me *one*." And suiting the action to the word, he handed the infidel the Bible, repeating the challenge, "You say there are scores of contradictions in the Bible, show me just *one*." Suffice it to say, he could not. You can afford to challenge such an objector with the same test. Even if there were contradictions in the Bible, such a man is not the one to be in possession of the knowledge.

A good verse to use with such persons is, 2 Pet. 2:12:

> But these, as natural brute beasts, made to be taken and destroyed, speak evil of the things that they understand not; and shall utterly perish in their own corruption.

3. "The Bible is an impure book."

It is difficult to know how one can make such a charge against a book that has done more for the production of purity of character than any other force in the world. The best and purest characters in the world are lovers and constant readers of the Bible.

It is sufficient, so far as the allegation itself is concerned, to label it as a lie. But the inquirer must be dealt with. His sincerity may be instantly questioned. He is in need of a straight talk.

Show him Psa. 12:6, and 119:140:

> The words of the Lord are pure words: as silver tried in a furnace of earth, purified seven times.
> Thy word is very pure: therefore thy servant loveth it.

Also Prov. 30:5.

From these passages we learn that the Bible is a pure book—pure from the beginning to the end.

It is a good thing to send an arrow of conviction into the soul of the objector, and show him where the real cause of the trouble lies. This may be done by using Prov. 30:12. Also

Titus 1 :15:

> Unto the pure all things are pure: but unto them
> that are defiled and unbelieving is nothing pure; but
> even their mind and conscience is defiled.

and 2 Pet. 2 :11, 12.

The impurity lies not in the Bible, but in his own
wicked heart.

4. "The Bible is a mere human book."

One of the best passages in the Bible to use in dealing with this class is

1 Thess. 2 :13:

> For this cause also thank we God without ceasing, be-
> cause, when ye received the word of God which ye
> heard of us, ye received it not as the word of men, but,
> as it is in truth, the word of God, which effectually
> worketh also in you that believe.

It is here definitely stated that the Bible is not the
word of man, but the Word of the living God.

2 Pet. 1 :20, 21:

> Knowing this first, that no prophecy of the scripture
> is of any private interpretation.
> For the prophecy came not in old time by the will of
> man: but holy men of God spake as they were moved
> by the Holy Ghost.

It is clear from the context that this passage refers
to the origin rather than to the exposition of the
Scriptures. The Bible is not a mere product of the
human mind.

2 Tim. 3 :16 shows us that the Bible is the result of
divine inbreathing.

THOSE WHO FIND FAULT WITH CHRISTIANS AND
CHURCH MEMBERS.

One of the most frequent excuses offered in the inquiry room is this one which finds its basis in the

inconsistency of professing Christians.   It assumes various forms, as for example:

1. "There are too many hypocrites in the church."

How shall we meet this objection? Admit its truth, for it is undoubtedly true. Ofttimes the admission comes with such unexpectedness to the inquirer that he is at once disarmed. It may be well to tell him that, while we are sorry that there are hypocrites in the church, and that we are doing our best to put them out, yet, there is no more reason for his keeping out of the church on this account than for his staying in the world, for there are hypocrites in the world. Sometimes one finds that an objector is a member of some society or lodge; you may then ask him, if there are any hypocrites in it, and if so, why he does not leave the lodge. This reveals to him the inconsistency of his argument.

Again, you may remind him that the existence of the false and counterfeit implies the existence of the true and genuine. The best, not the poorest Christians, should form the standard of judgment and comparison.

(a) Show him that he has no right to judge others, and that God will hold him responsible for so doing.

Rom. 14:4, 10:

> Who art thou that judgest another man's servant? to his own master he standeth or falleth. Yea, he shall be holden up: for God is able to make him stand.
> But why dost thou judge thy brother? or why dost thou set at nought thy brother? for we shall all stand before the judgment seat of Christ.

Also Rom. 2:1-3.

(b) Draw his attention to his own sin and inconsistency, and show him that God will hold him responsible for that, and not for the inconsistencies of others

Rom. 2:1, 21-23:

> Therefore thou art inexcusable, O man, whosoever thou art that judgest: for wherein thou judgest another, thou condemnest thyself; for thou that judgest doest the same things.
>
> Thou therefore which teachest another, teachest thou not thyself? thou that preachest a man should not steal, dost thou steal?
>
> Thou that sayest a man should not commit adultery, dost thou commit adultery? thou that abhorrest idols, dost thou commit sacrilege?
>
> Thou that makest thy boast of the law, through breaking the law dishonourest thou God?

Also Matt. 7:1-5 and Rom. 14:12.

It is very probable, as Rom. 2:1 says, that he himself is guilty of the very sin of which he is accusing others.

(c) Show him that, if he knows how Christians ought to live, God will hold him responsible for not living up to that light.

Luke 12:47, 48:

> And that servant, which knew his lord's will, and prepared not himself, neither did according to his will, shall be beaten with many stripes. But he that knew not, and did commit things worthy of stripes, shall be beaten with few stripes.

2. "Christians and church members do things I would not do."

It may be well to remind him that Christ, and not any church member, is the model after whom he is to pattern his life. A good passage for this purpose is John 21:21, 22:

> Peter seeing him, saith to Jesus, Lord, and what shall this man do?
>
> Jesus saith unto him, If I will that he tarry till I come, what is that to thee? follow thou me.

Also Matt. 23:10 and Jer. 2:5.

It may be well, in closing this case, to show the inquirer the despicableness of such a fault-finding disposition that leads him to pass over all the virtues and dwell upon the faults of Christians—not the strongest, but the weakest. A cat may be so intent upon watching a hole for a mouse that it fails to see an elephant as it passes by. So a man may be so intent upon finding fault that he fails to see virtues. There are people "that make a man an offender for a word . . . and turn aside the just for a thing of nought" (Isa. 29:21). Remind him that it will profit him more to spend a little time here, if necessary, with the hypocrites in the church rather than to spend an eternity with them in hell; for finally, when God shall separate the righteous—for he will certainly make that separation some day—from the wicked, all hypocrites, within and without the church, shall be cast into hell. "God shall appoint him his portion with the hypocrites; there shall be weeping and gnashing of teeth" (Matt. 24:51).

3. "Christians have treated me wrongly."

Ask him what fault he has to find with God's treatment of him. For this use

Micah 6:3:

> O my people, what have I done unto thee? and wherein have I wearied thee? testify against me.

And Isa. 5:3, 4, and Jer. 2:5.

Show him that God's dealings with him have been faultless; that he has received undeserved blessings from His hand, all of which have been designed to lead him to repentance. Use

Rom. 2:4:

> Or despisest thou the riches of his goodness and forbearance and longsuffering; not knowing that the goodness of God leadeth thee to repentance?

Also Psa. 103:10.

THOSE WHO FIND FAULT WITH THE CHRISTIAN LIFE.

1. "It is too hard and exacting."

Use Prov. 13:15:

> Good understanding giveth favour: but the way of transgressors is hard.

This verse tells us that it is the life of the sinner that is a hard one, and filled with many snares and dangers.

The life of the Christian is described in the following passages:

Prov. 3:17:

> Her ways are ways of pleasantness, and all her paths are peace.

1 John 5:3 and Prov. 4:18:

> But the path of the just is as the shining light, that shineth more and more unto the perfect day.

2. "It is unreasonable in its demands."

The following passages are useful in meeting this objection:

Deut. 10:12, 13:

> And now, Israel, what doth the Lord thy God require of thee, but to fear the Lord thy God, to walk in all his ways, and to love him, and to serve the Lord thy God with all thy heart and with all thy soul,
> To keep the commandments of the Lord, and his statutes, which I command thee this day for thy good?

Also Isa. 1:18· Micah 6:8.

THOSE WHO FIND FAULT WITH THE PLAN OF SALVA-
TION.

Ofttimes the person who is being dealt with finds fault with the means which God has ordained for the salvation of men. In answering this objection, the following scriptures will be helpful:

Rom. 9:19-21:

> Thou wilt say then unto me, Why doth he yet find fault? For who hath resisted his will?
>
> Nay but, O man, who art thou that repliest against God? Shall the thing formed say to him that formed it, Why hast thou made me thus?
>
> Hath not the potter power over the clay, of the same lump to make one vessel unto honour, and another unto dishonour?

Isa. 55:8, 9:

> For my thoughts are not your thoughts, neither are your ways my ways, saith the Lord.
>
> For as the heavens are higher than the earth, so are my ways higher than your ways and my thoughts than your thoughts.

Also Rom. 11:33, 34; 1 Cor. 1:26, 27.

THOSE WHO ARE MISLED
        BY ERRONEOUS VIEWS
              OF THE TRUTH

CHAPTER XIII.

IX.   THOSE WHO ARE MISLED BY ERRONEOUS VIEWS OF THE TRUTH.

1. The Roman Catholic.

TO deal effectively with the Roman Catholic, the personal worker must know what the Roman church believes and teaches, and in what respects it differs from Protestantism. It is well, also, to know what both churches believe in common. Some of the fundamental doctrines of the Christian faith are held in common by both these churches. Indeed, it is asserted by some that the main difference between the two denominations lies not so much in the matter of faith, as in the means by which the grace of God is to be brought to the hearts of men: the Romanist believing that it can come to the individual heart only through the agency of the church, while the Protestant claims that it comes from Christ directly through an act of faith on the part of the individual himself.

The wise Christian worker will not attack the Roman church in his conversation and dealing with the inquirer. This is likely to enrage the man, and make all successful dealing with him impossible. Indeed, it might be well to say what good you can about the Roman church. It is not wise under ordinary, if any, circumstances to arouse the antagonism of an inquirer unnecessarily; nothing is ever gained by it.

If you ask the Roman Catholic whether he is a Christian, he will doubtless answer in the affirmative. He may tell you that he has been baptized, or confirmed, or both, and that therefore he is a Christian.

It would be unwise for you to contradict him. Take it for granted, as a basis on which to begin your dealing with him, that he is a Christian, and ask him if he enjoys assurance of salvation. This leads to the first point under our dealing with the Roman Catholic.

(a) Begin by asking the inquirer if he enjoys the assurance of salvation.

This is beginning along the lines of least resistance. The Roman church, as such, from the most humble member thereof, even up to the Pope himself, does not pretend to enjoy the blessing of the assurance of salvation. Indeed, the church does not believe in its possibility; branding all such belief as religious presumption; claiming that no man can know he is saved until he gets to heaven.

You can use such passages as 1 John 5:13 to show that it is the will of God, according to the teaching of the Bible, that we should know that we are saved:

> These things have I written unto you that believe on the name of the Son of God; that ye may know that ye have eternal life, and that ye may believe on the name of the Son of God.

Also, 1 John 1:9; Acts 10:43; Acts 13:38, 39; Romans 8:14, 16; John 3:36; 5:24.

By the use of these scriptures you can show the inquirer that he may know that the various phases of Christian experience: the assurance of sins forgiven, the possession of eternal life and the knowledge of assured security are not only possible possessions of the Christian, but something that is demanded by the Word of God.

(b) Show the necessity of the new birth.

(1) Baptism and regeneration.

Ask him if he has been "born again"; if he has become "a new creature" in Christ Jesus. He will doubtless tell you that he was born again when, as an infant, he was baptized (for the Roman church believes that regeneration takes place in baptism).

It will be well to show him from the Scriptures that baptism is not regeneration, although it is often mistaken for it. This may be done by the use of two passages in the First Epistle to the Corinthians.

In 1 Cor. 4:15, the apostle says:

> For though ye have ten thousand instructors in Christ, yet have ye not many fathers: for in Christ Jesus I have begotten you through the gospel.

By this he means to say that they were regenerated through his agency; that the Holy Spirit used him as the instrument through which they were led to a saving knowledge of Jesus Christ. This is the clear teaching of this passage.

Now, in 1 Cor. 1:14, the apostle further says:

> I thank God that I baptized none of you, but Crispus and Gaius.

In this passage the apostle seems to depreciate the rite of baptism so far as it being an agency in their regeneration is concerned. Could he possibly have thus treated baptism if it had been an essential element in their regeneration?

The case of Simon Magus (Acts 8:9-24), who was baptized by the apostles, but who, as the context clearly shows, still remained unconverted and was yet "in the gall of bitterness, and the bond of iniquity," may be used to show that baptism is not to be substituted for the new birth

(2) Regeneration defined.

From 2 Cor. 5:17:

> Therefore if any man be in Christ, he is a new creature: old things are passed away; behold, all things are become new.

and Gal. 6:15, show what regeneration is: that it does not consist in the observance of any mere outward ceremonial act, such as baptism or confirmation, but that it is becoming "a new creature" (or creation); the dying to the old life of sin, and the rising to a new life of righteousness (1 John 5:4).

Then show from John 1:12, 13; 1 John 5:1; 1 Peter 1:23, and Romans 10:9, 10, how a man is born again: by believing what the Word of God has to say about Jesus Christ, receiving Him thus as one's own personal Saviour, and confessing Him as such a Saviour before the world.

(3) Evidences of the new birth.

Show the inquirer the marks by which he may know that he has been born again. This may be done by the use of many references in 1 John:

5:4—"overcometh the world";

3:9—victory over sin;

3:14—"love of the brethren," etc.

In this connection it might be well to distinguish between confirmation and regeneration. The Romanist often mistakes the one for the other. Mere reformation is not regeneration. Such scriptures as Matthew 7:21-23; Luke 11:24-26:

> When the unclean spirit is gone out of a man, he walketh through dry places, seeking rest; and finding none, he saith, I will return unto my house, whence I came out.
> And when he cometh he findeth it swept and garnished.

and 13:25, 26, show conclusively that one may reform in life and yet not be a true Christian, and finally fail of entering heaven.

(c) True repentance necessary.

In dealing with the Roman Catholic, emphasis needs to be laid upon the necessity of true repentance. Too often he is satisfied with the mere confession of his sins to the priest, forgetting that no confessed sin is forgiven unless it is at the same time forsaken. Repentance is not only a heart broken *for* sin; it is also a heart broken *from* sin. Such passages as Proverbs 28:13; Jonah 3:10; and Isaiah 55:7 clearly enforce this duty.

The sole mediatorship of Jesus Christ is a fact that needs to be strongly emphasized. 1 Timothy 2:5 is a good passage to use in this connection:

> For there is one God, and one mediator between God and men, the man Christ Jesus.

Also Acts 4:12.

(d) Get the Roman Catholic to read the Bible.

Finally, it is a good thing, if you can do it, to get the Roman Catholic to carefully read his Bible. It matters not very much whether it be the Catholic or Protestant Version. Probably more Catholics have been led to Christ in this way than in any other. I remember receiving into the membership of my church a young man who had been for many years a French Roman Catholic. I asked him how he came to renounce Roman Catholicism for Protestantism. He told me that one evening he wandered into a prayer meeting, and listened to the testimonies of saved men and women. He was deeply impressed with the joyful assurance that marked the testimonies, and resolved that he would find out the secret of it. He confessed that he himself was a stranger to such an experience, although a member of the church. In speaking with one of those who had testified, at the close of the meeting, his attention was directed to the Bible. He resolved that he would own a Protestant Bible for himself. He purchased one, and read it night after night on his return from work, hiding it safely afterwards so that his parents would not know what he was reading. After some weeks of such reading and study of the Scriptures, he came to the conclusion that such an experience was for him too. So, in his room, he knelt and definitely surrendered his life to God. From that time forward he knew the joy of the Lord. It was the reading of the Word of God that did it. "The entrance of Thy Word giveth light."

2. The Unitarian.

Generally speaking, a Unitarian is one who denies the doctrine of the Trinity; *i. e.,* he believes in God the Father, but not in God the Son, or in God the Holy Ghost. More specifically, Unitarianism regards Christ as a very good and holy, indeed, the best man, but by no means divine and equal with the Father. The Holy Spirit is looked upon rather as an influence than a person, and, most certainly, not a divine person. The Bible is regarded as a work of great genius, yet not inspired and infallible, nor as the ultimate authority in matters of faith and practice. The miracles of the Bible are explained on a naturalistic basis, somewhat mythical, and of the nature of folklore. The atonement and regeneration are both disbelieved, the terms scarcely ever being used by them. Sin is more of a defect of human nature than a thing of guilt; something that may be removed by culture and education. There are, however, here and there, especially in the New England states, some Unitarians who are not so radical as this, and whose beliefs resemble somewhat the orthodox faith, except, of course, in the matter of the doctrine of the Trinity.

The main point at issue, however, with which the personal worker will have to deal, will be the relation of the Unitarian to the person and work of Christ. Other things will adjust themselves if this fundamental doctrine is satisfactorily dealt with. We cannot think

aright in the rest unless we think rightly of Him.
Someone has well said,

> Names, and sects, and parties fall;
> But Thou, O Christ, art all in all.

(a) Show him that he cannot have the Father without the Son.

1 John 2:22, 23 is very explicit on this matter:

> Who is a liar but he that denieth that Jesus is the
> Christ? He is antichrist, that denieth the Father and
> the Son.
> Whosoever denieth the Son, the same hath not the
> Father; but he that acknowledgeth the Son, hath the
> Father also.

In John 14:6 we have a distinct and positive affirma.
tion that access to the Father is obtainable only
through Jesus Christ the Son.

In Matthew 11:27, the Lord Jesus Himself says:

> All things are delivered unto me of my Father; and
> no man knoweth the Son, but the Father; neither
> knoweth any man the Father, save the Son, and he
> to whomsoever the Son will reveal him.

To disown the Son is to shut the door of knowledge
that opens to the Father in one's own face. Any professed faith in the Father, and assumed knowledge or
communion with Him to which the Unitarian may lay
claim, is, according to these scriptures, shown to be
false and ungrounded. These are startling assertions.

*(b) Show that salvation comes in no other way, save
through the person and work of Jesus Christ.*

Acts 4:12 is uncompromising in its assertion of this
tremendous fact:

> Neither is there salvation in any other: for there is
> none other name under heaven given among men, whereby
> we must be saved.

Can words be clearer in their meaning than these?
Does not the refusal to believe in Christ mean the
virtual rejection of a proffered salvation? Are any

words of Christ Himself more final and decisive than
those found in John 8:21, 24?

> Then said Jesus again unto them, I go my way, and ye
> shall seek me, and shall die in your sins: whither I go,
> ye cannot come.
> I said therefore unto you, that ye shall die in your
> sins: for if ye believe not that I am he, ye shall die in
> your sins.

The attitude of the Unitarian of today is practically
that of the Jews of our Lord's day to whom these
words were spoken.

*(c) Show that it most certainly is the will of God
the Father that men should believe on the name of
His Son, Jesus Christ.*

This is clear from such passages as John 5:22, 23:

> For the Father judgeth no man, but hath committed all
> judgment unto the Son;
> That all men should honor the Son, even as they honor
> the Father. He that honoreth not the Son honoreth
> not the Father which hath sent him.

Also Phil. 2:9.

*(d) Show the awful guilt resting upon the man who
rejects Jesus Christ as his Saviour.*

You may emphasize the fact that unbelief in Christ
is the greatest sin in the world, as taught in John
16:8-10:

> And when he is come, he will reprove the world of
> sin, and of righteousness, and of judgment:
> Of sin, because they believe not on me;
> Of righteousness, because I go to my Father, and ye
> see me no more.

This is the one sin above all others of which the Holy
Spirit has come into the world to convict men.

1 John 2:22, 23 may be used to show that the sin
of refusal to accept Jesus Christ is nothing more or
less than the possession of the spirit of Antichrist.

1 John 5:10-12 shows that to thus reject Jesus Christ
as the One through whom the Father bestows eternal
life is to charge God with being a liar:

He that believeth on the Son of God hath the witness in himself: he that believeth not God hath made him a liar; because he believeth not the record that God gave of his Son.

And this is the record, that God hath given to us eternal life, and this life is in his Son.

He that hath the Son hath life; and he that hath not the Son of God hath not life.

Another good passage is Heb. 10:28, 29. Than these, there are no more solemn words in the Bible. The sin in these verses which brings down upon the head of the one committing it such dreadful consequences, is the denial of the claim of Jesus Christ, and the accounting of the blood of the atonement simply of the nature of the death of any martyr. Is not this the sin which Unitarianism is committing?

(e) If the inquirer seeks to have you prove to him from the Scriptures that Jesus Christ is Deity, the Son of God, the Saviour of the world, show him:

(1) That divine names are given to Jesus Christ.

Acts 3:14:

But ye denied the Holy One and the Just, and desired a murderer to be granted unto you.

Also John 20:28; Heb. 1:8, and Titus 2:13.

(2) Divine attributes ascribed to Him.
Omnipotence. He can do all things:

Matt. 28:18:

And Jesus came and spake unto them, saying, All power is given unto me in heaven and in earth.

Also Eph. 1:22, 23.

Omniscience. He knows all things:

Mark 2:8:

And immediately when Jesus perceived in his spirit that they so reasoned within themselves, he said unto them, Why reason ye these things in your hearts?

Also Col. 2:3; John 2:24-25; 4:16-19; 6:64; 16:30.

Omnipresence.   He is everywhere.

Matt. 18:20 :

> For where two or three are gathered together in my name, there am I in the midst of them.

Also John 14:20; 3:13; Eph. 1:23.

Eternity.   He always existed.

John 1:1 :

> In the beginning was the Word, and the Word was with God, and the Word was God.

Also John 8:58; Micah 5:2; Heb. 13:8; John 1:2.

(3) Divine works ascribed to Him.

Creation.

John 1:1-3 :

> The beginning was the Word, and the Word was with God, and the Word was God.
> The same was in the beginning with God.
> All things were made by him; and without him was not any thing made that was made.

Also Col. 1:16 :

> For by him were all things created, that are in heaven, and that are in earth, visible and invisible, whether they be thrones, or dominions, or principalities, or powers; all things were created by him, and for him.

Also Heb. 1:10; John 1:1-3.

Judgment.

John 5:22, 23 :

> For the Father judgeth no man, but hath committed all judgment unto the Son:
> That all men should honor the Son, even as they honor the Father. He that honoreth not the Son honoreth not the Father which hath sent him.

John 6:39 :

> And this is the Father's will which hath sent me, that of all which he hath given me I should lose nothing, but should raise it up again at the last day.

Also John 5:28, 29.

Gives eternal life.

John 5:21:

> For as the Father raiseth up the dead, and quickeneth them; even so the Son quickeneth whom he will.

Also John 10:27, 29.

(4) Divine worship is accorded to Him.

Matt. 28:9:

> And as they went to tell his disciples, behold, Jesus met them, saying, All hail. And they came and held him by the feet, and worshipped him.

Matt. 14:33:

> Then they that were in the ship came and worshipped him, saying, Of a truth thou art the Son of God.

Also Luke 24:52; Rev. 22:8, 9; Psa. 45:11; John 5:23, with Rev. 5:8, 9, 12, 13; Heb. 1:6; Phil. 2:10, 11.

3. The Universalist.

By the Universalist is meant one who claims that every one is going to be finally saved; that no created being will be forever lost.

HOW TO DEAL WITH THEM.

(a) Know and understand the scriptures on which they base their argument.

They are as follows:

1 Tim. 2:3, 4:

> For this is good and acceptable in the sight of God our Saviour;
> Who will have all men to be saved, and to come unto the knowledge of the truth.

You may show them that this passage teaches not the determined purpose and decree of God, but the

desire and wish on the part of God that all men should
be saved.   To desire and wish the salvation of a person
is not the same as determining that that thing shall
take place.   God does not determine that all men shall
be saved, but *desires* that all men *should* be saved.
Matthew 1:19 illustrates both uses of the word *will*:

1 Cor. 15:22:

> For as in Adam all die, even so in Christ shall all be
> made alive.

This verse deals not with the question of all men
receiving eternal life in Christ, but with the physical
resurrection of all men because of Christ's resurrection.
The whole race died *physically* in Adam; the whole
race rises *physically* in Christ.   This is the clear interpretation according to the context.

*(b) Show that the will of man has some part to play
in his salvation.*

For example, he must *repent* (Luke 13:3); he must
believe (John 3:36); he must *forsake his sins* (Prov.
28:13); he must *come to Christ* (John 5:40).

*(c) Use such passages as show that all men are not
saved.*

Matt. 25:41-46:

> Then shall he say also unto them on the left hand,
> Depart from me, ye cursed, into everlasting fire, pre-
> pared for the devil and his angels:
> For I was an hungred, and ye gave me no meat; I was
> thirsty, and ye gave me no drink:
> I was a stranger, and ye took me not in: naked, and
> ye clothed me not: sick, and in prison, and ye visited
> me not.
> Then shall they also answer him, saying, Lord, when
> saw we thee an hungred, or athirst, or a stranger, or
> naked, or sick, or in prison, and did not minister unto
> thee?
> Then shall he answer them, saying, Verily I say unto
> you, Inasmuch as ye did it not to one of the least of
> these, ye did it not to me.
> And these shall go away into everlasting punishment:
> but the righteous into life eternal.

Compare also Rev. 20:15; 21:8; 2 Thess. 1:7-9.

4. The Seventh-Day Adventist.

In dealing with this class, the Christian worker should seek to acquaint himself quite fully with what Seventh-Day Adventists believe. The following booklets will give much of the desired information: *Ought Christians to Keep the Sabbath?* by R. A. Torrey; *Adventism Refuted*, by D. M. Canright; *Seventh-Day Adventism*, by David Anderson Berry.

The fundamental doctrine of Seventh-Day Adventism is the absolute necessity of keeping the seventh day of the week (Saturday) as the Sabbath. Those who do not keep Saturday as the Sabbath, but, instead, keep Sunday (the first day of the week) have upon them the mark of the beast, and, therefore, cannot be saved.

How to Deal With Them.

(a) Know their favorite passages, and show how they wrongly interpret them.

1 John 2:4:

> He that saith, I know him, and keepeth not his commandments, is a liar, and the truth is not in him.

The commandment in this verse is made to mean the Sabbath. They make an almost constant practice of reading the word "Sabbath" in place of the word "commandment" wherever such word occurs in the New Testament. By the use of 1 John 3:23:

> And this is his commandment, That we should believe on the name of his Son Jesus Christ, and love one another, as he gave us commandment.

you can show what God means by the commandments of Christ: love and faith, not Sabbath-keeping.

Another favorite passage with the Adventist is Rev. 22:14:

> Blessed are they that do his commandments, that they may have right to the tree of life, and may enter in through the gates into the city.

The "commandments" here, of course, are made to mean the Ten Commandments, which naturally includes the fourth, or the Sabbath-keeping commandment. Participation in eternal life is, therefore, said to be dependent upon keeping this commandment. A careful reading of this verse in the Revised Version will show that the words "that keep his commandments" are omitted entirely from the text. So there is nothing left for the Adventist to build his doctrine on in this verse.

(b) Show them that the Law (on tables of stone, clearly the so-called moral law) is done away.

2 Cor. 3:7-11:

> But if the ministration of death, written and engraven in stones, was glorious, so that the children of Israel could not steadfastly behold the face of Moses for the glory of his countenance; which glory was to be done away;
> How shall not the ministration of the spirit be rather glorious?
> For if the ministration of condemnation be glory, much more doth the ministration of righteousness exceed in glory.
> For even that which was made glorious had no glory in this respect, by reason of the glory that excelleth.
> For if that which is done away was glorious, much more that which remaineth is glorious.

The Sabbath was one of the laws written on the tables of stone. These, Scripture says, were "done away." In these verses we have a distinct statement that the covenant that was represented by the two tables of stone upon which was written the Sabbath law is abolished. You are therefore placed on the horns of a dilemma, either you are under the Old Covenant with its ministration of death, or you are under the New Covenant with its ministration of the Spirit who giveth life. If you keep the seventh-day Sabbath, you are acknowledging that you are under the former, and therefore have no claim to the benefits of the latter. Not only so, but as to be under the former necessitates your becoming a Jew; so the Seventh-Day Adventist dictum is: "Gentile Christians must become Israelites, and so come under the obligation to keep the Sabbath, for the Sabbath was given forever throughout their generations."

(c) Show them that by the death of Christ Christians have become dead to the Law.

Rom. 7:1-4:

> Know ye not, brethren, (for I speak to them that know the law,) how that the law hath dominion over a man as long as he liveth?
>
> For the woman which hath a husband is bound by the law to her husband so long as he liveth; but if the husband be dead, she is loosed from the law of her husband.
>
> So then if, while her husband liveth, she be married to another man, she shall be called an adulteress: but if her husband be dead, she is free from that law; so that she is no adulteress, though she be married to another man.
>
> Wherefore, my brethren, ye also are become dead to the law by the body of Christ; that ye should be married to another, even to him who is raised from the dead, that we should bring forth fruit unto God.

Compare with this Rom. 10:3-9.

(d) Show them that every one of the Ten Commandments, except the fourth, referring to Sabbath observance, is reaffirmed in the New Testament.

There is no hint anywhere that the Sabbath law is binding on the Christian. By the example of Christ. the contrary seems to be the case. (Compare the discussion regarding the disciples plucking corn on the Sabbath day, Matt. 12:1-8.) Indeed, Christ seems to consider the Sabbath law less binding than any other one of the ten, for He says it may be broken under certain circumstances and the breaker yet be guiltless. This could not be true of covetousness, or adultery, even though such a sin were committed within the sacred precincts of the temple. Indeed, it would be all the more grievous because committed therein.

(e) Show them that the Sabbath obligation is expressly and plainly declared not to be binding upon the Christian.

Col. 2:16, 17:

> Let no man therefore judge you in meat, or in drink, or in respect of a holyday, or of the new moon, or of the sabbath days:
> Which are a shadow of things to come: but the body is of Christ.

Seventh-Day Adventists may here contend that Paul did not refer to the regular *weekly* Sabbath, but to some one of the *special* Sabbaths. Why did he not say so then?

Indeed, does he not refer to such special Sabbaths by calling them feasts, new-moons, etc.? (Compare 2 Chron. 2:4; 8:13.) Paul includes in his category all these shadowy Sabbaths, as they are called, as well as the weekly Sabbath. This has been illustrated as follows: You are standing in the road with your back to the rising sun; suddenly the shadow of a hat appears, and as it passes you the head next appears, and so on. By this you know someone is overtaking you; but owing to the position of the sun the shadow is long drawn out, and some moments may elapse ere your friend in the body overtakes you. So Christ was coming, and, unseen, cast His shadow before in the form of Old Testament rites and ceremonies, holy days, new-moons, and Sabbaths. But when He who cast the shadow came, it would surely be foolish to be occupied with the shadow and not with Himself. And now He is gone awhile, we need no shadow, for we have the substance in the third person in the Holy Trinity, who dwells with us and in us as the representative of our absent Lord Jesus. This, those who lived under the old dispensation, the economy of shadows, had not.

(f) Show that the Sabbath is a purely Jewish institution and was never meant to be binding on the Christian.

This is clearly stated in the following passages; note the context of each.

Deut. 5:12-15:

Here the Sabbath is used in connection with the deliverance from Egypt—*"Therefore* the Lord thy God commanded thee to keep the Sabbath day."

See also Ex. 20:1, 2, and note context.

The Sabbath was a sign between Israel and God (Ex. 31:13-17; Ezek. 20:12, 13). It is true the Sabbath is mentioned in Gen. 2:3, but it is not mentioned there as a command or a law, but wherever it is given as a law it is in connection with Israel. When Israel as a nation passed away, that Sabbath passed away; when Israel shall again be restored, then the Sabbath and its obligations shall again be binding. This is just what we find in Isa. 52:2-7. We must distinguish between the Jew, the Gentile, and the Church of God (1 Cor. 10:32). The Christian is not a child of Israel, he is a child of God, with a place in the Body of Christ, where no national distinctions are known—"neither Jew nor Gentile."

(g) Show them that it is impossible for even an Adventist to keep the Jewish Sabbath; so that, if this were required, a Seventh-Day Adventist could not be saved.

According to their teaching, a believer who fails to keep the Sabbath is lost.

Here is the Adventist's position on the Sabbath-keeping question:

(1) The observance of the Sabbath from sunset on Friday to sunset on Saturday.

(2) The non-observance of this is "the mark of the beast."

(3) There is no hope of salvation for those who will not keep the Sabbath.

(4) Through the two great errors, the immortality of the soul and Sunday sacredness, Satan will bring the people under his deceptions.

(5) Sabbath-keeping is the great sign of loyalty to God, for it is written: "It is a sign between me and the children of Israel forever."

(6) Believers who fail to keep the Sabbath are lost; for Mrs. White, a noted Seventh-Day Adventist author, says: "If it is seen that, though running well for a time, they did not overcome (*i. e.*, kept not the Sabbath), then instead of confessing their names before the Father and His angels, and blotting out their sins, Christ will blot out their names from the book of life . . . after which Christ will come to take to Himself those who are found to be loyal to Him."

But can and do the Seventh-Day Adventists keep the Sabbath according to Jewish law? Let us see. Take this quotation from their catechism:

"*Q.* In Ex. 35:3 we read: Ye shall kindle no fire throughout your habitation upon the Sabbath day."

Do they obey this? If not, how do they get around it? In this way:

"*A. In that climate fire was not needed for warmth, and the very fact that one was kindled indicated that unnecessary labor was to be performed.*"

Here is extreme and inexcusable ignorance. What does the very Book they profess to study say? John

18:18: "And the servants and officers stood there who had made a fire of coals, *for it was cold;* and they *warmed* themselves; and Peter stood with them and *warmed* himself." If Christians are thus required to keep the Sabbath, how then can they live in cold climates?

Again, Israel kept their Sabbath from sunset, Friday, to sunset, Saturday. The law is clear upon the point: "From even unto even shall ye celebrate your Sabbath." They could do this with the utmost regularity in their own land. But what happens in those lands where there are no sunsets at certain seasons of the year. How about such countries as Norway and Sweden? Further, how do you explain the fact that far away towards the extremes of the earth, traveling from the equator, there are periods of six months day and six months night from age to age? Do you not see that it is a geographical impossibility for all men to keep the same day, and that the Sabbath law, so far as its obedience to the letter is concerned, was only intended for one people, one country, and one age?

(*h*) *Show that the commandment in the Decalogue is to keep the Sabbath—the seventh day.*

But there is no established starting point from which to count. Again, it would be impossible for all the world to have the same starting point.

A Seventh-Day Adventist thought to confuse Dr. Torrey by asking: "One of the commandments says, 'The seventh day is the Sabbath day of the Lord,' and yet Sunday is observed instead. Has God changed?"

Dr. Torrey's reply must have confused the questioner, for he said:

"The Bible doesn't say the seventh day of the week is the Sabbath of the Lord; the Sabbath was the seventh day—after they had labored six days. God was not guilty of any such folly as giving a law that it would be impossible to keep. If our being saved depended upon a certain section of the week, I should estimate that at least half the Seventh-Day Adventists would be lost; for, while Seventh-Day Adventists in Australia are observing Sabbath, the great body of their fellow-believers are working just as hard as they know how, for the seventh day doesn't come in Chicago, where I live, until sixteen hours after it comes here. Now, which section is saved, and which is lost? Again, I started from America last December, and on my way here I crossed the 180th meridian, in doing which I lost my Thursday, and ever since I have been keeping Saturday. Even then I don't keep it as the seventh day—I do it as the first day. Suppose two Seventh-Day Adventists started to go round the world—one east, the other west, each keeping Saturday. By the time they met, there would be two days' difference between them. Can you tell me which of them would be saved?"

(i) Seventh-Day Adventists deny the conscious existence of the soul after death; they believe that the soul sleeps between death and the resurrection.

According to this teaching, there is no comforting outlook for the believer. As it happeneth to the beast, so it happeneth to the man—they both go to the one place. How contrary this is to the teaching of the Bible! Compare 2 Cor. 5:1-8; Phil. 1:20-23.

It is of importance in dealing with this class to know on what Scriptural basis they found their belief in the sleep of the soul. We must be able to give the proper interpretation of these Scripture references. They are as follows:

Acts 2:34: "For David is not ascended into the heavens." This is their favorite text, or one of them. But the context shows clearly that it is the body and not the soul or spirit of David that is here spoken of:

compare "His sepulchre is with us," "He is both dead and buried," "He spake of the resurrection of Christ . . . that his body did not see corruption." (vv. 29, 31.)

Eccl. 9:5-10. "The dead know nothing," etc. This passage is limited by the context—"under the sun." Yet what does 2 Sam. 15:11 mean? "With Absalom went 200 men . . . they went in their simplicity, and *they knew not anything*." The context explains it—they knew nothing of Absalom's plot. Again 1 Sam. 20:39, as concerning the lad who ran after Jonathan's arrows: "But the lad *knew not anything;* only David and Jonathan knew the matter." So 1 Tim. 6:4, referring to a proud, self-conceited teacher, "He is proud, *knowing nothing*." Were all these without consciousness or without thought? No; but they knew nothing about *the things in particular mentioned*. So with Eccl. 9:6: "Neither have they a portion for ever in anything *that is done under the sun*."

Dan. 12:2 with John 11:11, 14, 39: "Those that sleep in the dust"; "Lazarus sleepeth."

Why not observe the words: "Lazarus is dead . . . he now stinketh"? Can these words be used of the spirit or soul of Lazarus? Certainly not.

So with 1 Thess. 4:16, 17.

This refers to the resurrection of the body, and not to the spirit. As the spirit does not go down into the grave at death (2 Cor. 5; Phil. 1:21-23), these verses can have no reference to it.

Matt. 27:52 explains the whole teaching of these passages,—that the reference is to the resurrection of the bodies and not to the sleep of the soul. "The *graves* were opened, and many *bodies* of the saints which *slept* arose. That is the sum and substance of it all—*graves, bodies, slept*.

(j) Show that the Scriptures teach that the spirit or soul does not die with the body.

Eccl. 12:7; 3:21; 1 Cor. 5:5; Luke 23:43, 46.

When Stephen died (and Jesus too) his body went down to the grave, but his spirit he committed into the hands of God (Acts 7:59).

According to 2 Cor. 12:2,—

> I knew a man in Christ above fourteen years ago, (whether in the body, I cannot tell; or whether out of the body, I cannot tell: God knoweth;) such a one caught up to the third heaven—

a man can live outside of his body and go to heaven. Refer to the story of the Rich Man and Lazarus, the burial of the body in the grave, and the conscious existence of the soul in another world (Luke 16:19-31). Here an intelligent conversation is carried on between the spirits of the departed. In the clearest possible way these passages teach the conscious state of the dead.

Matt. 10:28:

> And fear not them which kill the body, but are not able to kill the soul: but rather fear him which is able to destroy both soul and body in hell.

Then the soul does not die with the body, as is witnessed to by the appearance of Moses and Elijah on the transfiguration mount.

A fuller treatment of this subject will be found in *Ought Christians to Keep the Sabbath?* by Dr. R. A. Torrey.

5. The Spiritualist.

Spiritualism is the belief that disembodied spirits can and do communicate with the living, especially through the agency of a person particularly susceptible to spiritualistic influence called a "medium." Under the term "Spiritualism" are to be classed all the various doctrines and theories collectively founded upon this belief.

It professes to give advice spiritual, professional, and domestic. It boasts of being able to give tangible evidence of immortality so that we need not accept this great doctrine by faith alone.

Some have sought to explain the phenomena of Spiritualism on the basis of trickery, ventriloquism, or personal magnetism. Others claim that the whole thing is a huge fraud. A noted Spiritualist said: "Admit, if you will, that 99 per cent of Spiritualism is fraud, you must explain the hundredth part that is genuine and true."

A Christian worker should know how Spiritualism explains itself, and then how to meet it from the Bible.

(a) Show that Spiritualism denies the existence of Satan and angels.

Hence any communication between this and the invisible world must come from the spirits of departed human beings who move in circles around this earth, and are graded according to their moral qualities, the worst being nearest to us, and the best farthest from us.

(b) To expose the error of this doctrine, show that the Bible teaches that there is a class of beings in the invisible world distinct from the spirits of departed human beings.

Jude 6:

> And the angels which kept not their first estate, but left their own habitation, he hath reserved in everlasting chains, under darkness unto the judgment of the great day.

Also Heb. 12:22, 23.

From these scriptures we infer that there is an order of beings called angels, both good and bad. These verses cannot refer to men, for *all* men have sinned, whereas some of the angels did not sin; they do not refer to men, because these beings who sinned were cast down from heaven and out into darkness, and that is not true of man, for he has always been on the earth. Further, we are also told that the angels sang when the foundations of the world were laid, whereas man was not made until the sixth creative day. The passage in Hebrews clearly distinguishes between angels and the spirits of just men. It is clear from these passages that there is an order of beings wholly distinct from man, who are intelligent and have power to communicate with each other and with other intelligent beings, like man, if permitted to do so.

(c) Show that the work of their spirits is not the work of good angels.

The work of good angels is set forth in Hebrews 1:14. Such a helpful ministry as this is not the work of Spiritualism, for Spiritualism afflicts good people: it is skeptical, anti-Christian; it repudiates the Bible; it denies God.

(d) Show that Spiritualism is not the work of the spirits of the dead.

According to the Scriptures these are in heaven with Christ, and not roaming around the earth subject to the beck and call of any spiritualistic medium. We have no indications anywhere in the Bible that the spirits of departed ones communicate with the living on earth. Indeed, the parable of the Rich Man and Lazarus (Luke 16) shows the impossibility of such a revelation.

If, therefore, Spiritualism is not the work of good angels or of departed spirits, it must be the work of Satan and demons, and that is just what the Bible claims it to be.

1 Tim. 4:1:

Now the Spirit speaketh expressly, that in the latter times some shall depart from the faith, giving heed to seducing spirits, and doctrines of devils.

Compare also 2 Thess. 2:9-12, and 2 Tim. 3:13.

Dealing more specifically with Spiritualism,

(e) Endeavor to show the attitude of the Bible toward it. It is absolutely forbidden in the Scriptures.

Deut. 18:9-12:

> When thou art come into the land which the Lord thy God giveth thee, thou shalt not learn to do after the abominations of those nations.
> There shall not be found among you any one that maketh his son or his daughter to pass through the fire, or that useth divination, or an observer of times, or an enchanter, or a witch.
> Or a charmer, or a consulter with familiar spirits, or a wizard, or a necromancer.
> For all that do these things are an abomination unto the Lord: and because of these abominations the Lord thy God doth drive them out from before thee.

Compare also Lev. 19:31; Acts 16:16-18; Isa. 8:19-22.

(f) Show that God's curse rests upon it.

1 Chron. 10:13, 14:

> So Saul died for his transgression which he committed against the Lord, even against the word of the Lord, which he kept not, and also for asking counsel of one that had a familiar spirit, to inquire of it;
> And inquired not of the Lord: therefore he slew him, and turned the kingdom unto David the son of Jesse.

Compare also 2 Kings 21:1-6; Lev. 20:6; Deut. 18:10, 12; Rev. 21:8.

(g) Show that it is a repudiation of God's revelation in His Word.

Isa. 8:19, 20:

> And when they shall say unto you, Seek unto them that have familiar spirits, and unto wizards that peep and that mutter: should not a people seek unto their God? for the living to the dead?
> To the law and to the testimony: if they speak not according to this word, it is because there is no light in them.

Compare also Luke 16:27-31.

If in this connection the Spiritualist should refer **you** to the Bible story of the appearance of Samuel at **Endor** (1 Sam. 28 :11-20), you may show him that in this story Satan impersonates Samuel, for it cannot be that God, who had denied information to Saul in legitimate ways, would now grant that information in ways which met with His disapproval and upon which His curse rests.

(h) Finally, apply the Scriptural test by which we may know whether a doctrine is of God or not.

This test is found in 1 John 4 :1-3 :

> Beloved, believe not every spirit, but try the spirits whether they are of God : because many false prophets are gone out into the world.
> Hereby know ye the Spirit of God : Every spirit that confesseth that Jesus Christ is come in the flesh is of God :
> And every spirit that confesseth not that Jesus Christ is come in the flesh is not of God : and this is that spirit of antichrist, whereof ye have heard that it should come ; and even now already is it in the world.

The Scriptural test is the attitude towards Jesus Christ. Spiritualism denies the doctrines of Christ set forth in these verses, therefore Spiritualism is not of God : it is anti-Christian.

6. The Jew.

It is undoubtedly harder to lead a Jew than one of any other nationality to become a Christian. Work among the Jews has met with less numerical success than work among any other people. The principal objection of the Jew to the Christian religion is the acceptance of Jesus Christ as the Messiah and the Son of God. It is doubtless true that the fear of persecution also keeps many Jews from becoming Christians. These two thoughts must be kept prominent in the mind in dealing with these people. In dealing with the Jews, use the following method :

(a) Show from the Old Testament Scriptures that Jesus is the Christ.

This may be done by taking the words: "This was written that it might be fulfilled," as found in the Scriptures (in Matthew, for example), and referring to the events in the Old Testament which in this passage claim to have been fulfilled. Endeavor to show that the Christ of the New Testament, in whom all these things were fulfilled, was the promised Messiah of the Old Testament. One reason why Jews reject Jesus Christ as the Messiah is because of His humiliation and suffering, the which were considered by the Jews of our Lord's day, as they are considered by the Jews of our day, as being incompatible with the Messiahship. To show the falsity of this position you may refer to the 53rd chapter of Isaiah, the 22nd and 69th Psalms, and Zechariah 12:10—all of which are recognized as Messianic. From these you may show that the picture of Christ in the Old Testament was that of a suffering as well as a reigning Messiah.

(b) It will be well to show from the book of Hebrews how that the Old Testament sacrificial economy has been done away in Christ, and that salvation is now to be found only in the shed blood of Christ.

The 8th and 10th chapters of Hebrews in particular emphasize this truth.

(c) Show the nature of the punishment that comes because of the rejection of Jesus Christ as Saviour.

Some of the most solemn passages in the Bible deal with this phase of the question.

Heb. 10:26-29:

> For if we sin willfully after that we have received the knowledge of the truth, there remaineth no more sacrifice for sins,
> But a certain fearful looking for of judgment and fiery indignation, which shall devour the adversaries.
> He that despised Moses' law died without mercy under two or three witnesses:
> Of how much sorer punishment, suppose ye, shall he be thought worthy, who hath trodden under foot the Son of God, and hath counted the blood of the covenant, wherewith he was sanctified, an unholy thing, and hath done despite unto the Spirit of grace?

Compare also Heb. 6:4-6. Study these passages in the Revised Version

(d) If the fear of persecution is keeping the Jew from becoming a Christian, use the following scriptures:

2 Tim. 2:12:

> If we suffer, we shall also reign with him: if we deny him, he also will deny us:

Acts 5:40, 41:

> And to him they agreed: and when they had called the apostles, and beaten them, they commanded that they should not speak in the name of Jesus, and let them go.
> And they departed from the presence of the council, rejoicing that they were counted worthy to suffer shame for his name.

Compare also 2 Cor. 4:17; 1 Peter 2:20, 21.

7. The Christian Scientist.

In dealing with the Christian Science delusion, the Christian worker needs to guard against two things: underestimating it, or overestimating it. Its influence is subtle and far-reaching, but it is not so tremendously extensive and influential as many adherents of the sect would have us believe. The Christian need not be thrown into despair by any swelling reports of its teachings covering the whole world. "Christian Science is neither to be ridiculed nor feared; to be marvelled at nor tampered with, but examined and classified in the light of the only divine Revelation"—*James M. Gray.*

Neither should we be misled by the signs and wonders it professes to be able to perform. That these are not in themselves signs of their religion being from God is evident from the fact that such signs accompany the great apostasy of the latter days at whose head is Satan. Read Matt. 7:22, 23; 2 Thess. 2:8, 9; 2 Cor. 11:14, 15; Mark 13:22, 23. Pharoah's wise men

and astrologers were able to imitate God's servants, Moses and Aaron, by producing similar wonders.

The Christian worker should know in what respects Christian Science contradicts the Bible. "To the law and to the testimony: if they speak not acccording to this Word, it is because there is no light in them" (Isa. 8:20). The following arrangement, taken from *The Christian Science Delusion,* by Dr. A. C. Dixon, with his kind permission, sets before us in a concise way the teachings of Christian Science and the Bible contrasted (the quotations from *Science and Health* being of the edition of 1909) :

"Christian Science is a turning from the truth of revelation to the myths of imagination, as will appear by the following comparisons:

The Christian Science myth says:	The Truth of Revelation says:
The mere habit of pleading with the divine mind, as one pleads with a human being, perpetuates the belief in God as humanly circumscribed—an error which impedes spiritual growth. (p. 2.)	If ye then, being evil, know how to give good gifts unto your children, how much more shall your Father in heaven give good things to them that ask him? (Matt. 7:11.)
God is not influenced by man. (p. 7.)	Whatsoever ye shall ask in my name, that will I do, that the Father may be glorified in the Son. (John 14:13.)
One sacrifice, however great, is insufficient to pay the debt of sin. (p. 23.)	Now once in the end of the world hath he appeared to put away sin by the sacrifice of himself. (Heb. 9:26.)
The atonement requires constant self-immolation on the sinner's part. (p. 23.)	Being justified by faith, we have peace with God through our Lord Jesus Christ. (Rom. 5:1.)
Jesus' students, not sufficiently advanced fully to understand their Master's triumph, did not perform many wonderful works until they saw him after his crucifixion, and learned that he had not died. (pp. 45, 46.)	Christ both died and rose. (Rom. 14:9.)
This Comforter I understand to be Divine Science. (p. 55.)	I will pray the Father, and he shall give you another Comforter, that he may abide with you forever .... He shall teach you all things, and bring all things to your remembrance. (John 14:16, 26.)

The Christian Science myth:

The supposition that .... there are good and evil spirits is a mistake .... Evil has no reality. (pp. 70, 71.)

He restored Lazarus by the understanding that he never died. (p. 75.)

He never described disease. (p. 79.)

Miracles are impossible in science. (p. 83.)

Death is not a stepping-stone to life, immortality and bliss. (p. 203.)

Decrepitude is not according to law, nor is it a necessity of nature, but an illusion, that may be avoided. (1902 Edition, p. 245.)

God .... never created matter. (p. 335.)

The theory of three persons in one God—that is, a personal trinity—suggests p o l y t h e i s m (heathen gods, 1902 edition) rather than the ever-present I am. (p. 256.)

Man co-exists with God and the universe. (p. 266.)

In the infinitude of mind matter must be unknown (1902 Edition reads—Matter is unknown in the infinitude of mind. p. 280.)

Man has a sensationless body. (p. 280.)

Spirit and matter no more commingle than light and darkness; when one appears the other disappears. (p. 281.)

Truth demonstrated is eternal life. (p. 289.)

Heaven is not a locality. (p. 291.)

No final judgment awaits mortals. (p. 291.)

Evil is not made and is not real. (p. 311.)

The Truth of Revelation:

In that same hour he (Jesus) cured many .... of evil spirits. (Luke 7:21.)

Then said Jesus unto them plainly, Lazarus is dead. (John 11:14.)

Jesus .... rebuked the foul spirit, saying unto him, Thou dumb and deaf spirit. (Mark 9:25.)

Many believed in his name when they saw the miracles which he did. (John 2:23.)

To depart and be with Christ, which is far better. (Phil. 1:23.) Absent from the body, present with the Lord. (2 Cor. 5:8.)

The hoary head is a crown of glory, if it be found in the way of righteousness. (Prov. 16:31.)

In the beginning God created the heaven and the earth. (Gen. 1:1.)

Baptizing them in the name of the Father, and of the Son, and of the Holy Ghost. (Matt. 28:19.)

God created man. (Gen. 1:27.)

He is the saviour of the body. (Eph. 5:23.)

She felt in her body that she was healed. (Mark 5:29.)

Your body is the temple of the Holy Ghost. (1 Cor. 6:19.)

This is life eternal, that they might know thee the only true God, and Jesus Christ, whom thou hast sent. (John 17:3.)

I go to prepare a place for you. (John 14:2.)

It is appointed unto men once to die, but after this the judgment. (Heb. 9:27.)

Abhor that which is evil. (Rom. 12:9.)

It is a sense of sin, and not a sinful soul, which is lost. (p. 311.)

Because soul is immortal, soul cannot sin. (p. 468.)

The second appearance of Jesus is unquestionably the spiritual advent of the advancing idea of God in Christian Science. ("Autobiography," p. 96.)

What is a man profited, if he shall gain the whole world and lose his own soul? (Matt. 16:26.)

The soul that sinneth, it shall die. (Ezek. 18:4.)

I will come again. (John 14:3.) This same Jesus, which is taken up from you into heaven, shall so come in like manner as ye have seen him go into heaven. (Acts 1:11.)

DEALING SPECIFICALLY WITH THE CHRISTIAN SCIENTIST.

(1)   Christian Science virtually, indeed really, denies the personality of God.

It is true that its terms denying the personality of God are somewhat ambiguous, but in their final analysis they deny it. In commenting on 1 Tim. 2:3, 4, which reads as follows:

> For this is good and acceptable in the sight of God our Saviour; who will have all men to be saved, and to come unto the knowledge of the truth.

Christian Science says: "That which will have all men to be saved is principle, spirit, not person." It is considered by Christian Science authorities that no one can become an adept in that science, as a healer and teacher, without absolutely relinquishing the idea of a divine personality. Christian Science is, therefore, really pantheistic. It speaks of "the absolute allness of God"; God is good, good is God, truth is God, love is God. According to this, the answer of Christian Science to the question, "What is God?" is as follows: "God is not a person; God is mind or principle."

The Christian worker must show from the Scriptures that this idea of God is a false one. In the Bible, God is presented as a living God, who sees, who feels, has intelligence and power; who acts in behalf of His children, and who, by His providence, guides and controls in the affairs of men. The following passages may be used to set forth this truth:

Acts 14 :15 :

> And saying, Sirs, why do ye these things? We also
> are men of like passions with you, and preach unto you
> that ye should turn from these vanities unto the living
> God, which made heaven, and earth, and the sea, and all
> things that are therein.

Also 1 Thess. 1 :9 :

> For they themselves shew of us what manner of enter-
> ing in we had unto you, and how ye turned to God from
> idols to serve the living and true God.

See also Psalms 94 :9, 10; Jer. 10 :10-16.

*(2)   Christian Science denies the true doctrine of
Christ.*

(a)   It denies *His incarnation* by saying that "the
conception of Jesus was spiritual"—an idea, not a
person, conceived in the mind of the virgin whom she
called Jesus."

The Bible distinctly contradicts this statement.

Luke 1 :35 :

> And the angel answered and said unto her, The Holy
> Ghost shall come upon thee, and the power of the
> Highest shall overshadow thee : therefore also that holy
> thing which shall be born of thee shall be called the
> Son of God.

Indeed 1 John 4 :1-3 especially emphasizes the denial of the true person of Christ as a mark of the
antichrist :

> Beloved, believe not every spirit, but try the spirits
> whether they are of God: because many false prophets
> are gone out into the world.
> Hereby know ye the Spirit of God: Every spirit that
> confesseth that Jesus Christ is come in the flesh is
> of God.
> And every spirit that confesseth not that Jesus Christ
> is come in the flesh is not of God: and this is that
> spirit of antichrist, whereof ye have heard that it
> should come ; and even now already is it in the world.

In Christian Science, "Jesus" and "Christ" are separated.   "Christ" is supposed to be something of a
special anointing which came upon Jesus at His baptism and left Him at the cross.   This is flatly con-
tradicted by Scripture :

1 John 5:6-8:

> This is he that came by water and blood, even Jesus Christ; not by water only, but by water and blood. And it is the Spirit that beareth witness, because the Spirit is truth.
>
> For there are three that bear record in heaven, the Father, the Word, and the Holy Ghost: and these three are one.
>
> And there are three that bear witness in earth, the spirit, and the water, and the blood: and these three agree in one.

(b) Christian Science denies *the sacrificial effect of Christ's death.* Indeed, it practically denies the death of Christ altogether, by saying: "Jesus' students did not perform many wonderful works until they saw Him after the crucifixion, and learned that He had not died; He was merely fainting when pitying hands took Him down from the cross; His disciples believed Jesus dead when He was hidden in the sepulchre whereas He was alive."

This, of course, is contrary to the teaching of Scripture:

1 Cor. 15:1-4:

> Moreover, brethren, I declare unto you the gospel which I preached unto you, which also ye have received, and wherein ye stand;
>
> By which also ye are saved, if ye keep in memory what I preached unto you, unless ye have believed in vain.
>
> For I delivered unto you first of all that which I also received, how that Christ died for our sins according to the Scriptures;
>
> And that he was buried, and that he rose again the third day according to the Scriptures.

Also John 19:30-35:

> When Jesus therefore had received the vinegar, he said, It is finished: and he bowed his head, and gave up the ghost.
>
> The Jews therefore, because it was the preparation, that the bodies should not remain upon the cross on the sabbath day, (for that sabbath day was a high day,) besought Pilate that their legs might be broken, and that they might be taken away.
>
> Then came the soldiers, and brake the legs of the first, and of the other which was crucified with him.
>
> But when they came to Jesus, and saw that he was dead already, they brake not his legs:
>
> But one of the soldiers with a spear pierced his side, and forthwith came there out blood and water.

And he that saw it bare record, and his record is true; and he knoweth that he saith true, that ye might believe.

And Rom. 8:34; 14:15; 2 Cor. 5:14; 1 Thess. 4:14; Rom. 6:1-10.

(c)   Christian Science denies *the deity of Christ.*

Mrs. Eddy says, "Jesus was not God's son in any other sense than as every man is God's son."

This virtually makes no distinction between the divinity of Christ and the divinity of all men, whereas the Scriptures distinctly teaches that Jesus Christ was the Son of God, in a unique sense—a sense which cannot be predicated of any mere human being.   There never was a time when Jesus Christ was not the Son of God.   As a child He was *born,* but as a Son He was never born, but *given* (Isa. 9:6).   We, the sons of men, are the sons of God in a certain sense by creation, but there is another and a higher sense in which a man becomes a son of God the moment he believes in the Lord Jesus Christ.   See the following passages:

John 1:18:

No man hath seen God at any time; the only begotten Son, which is in the bosom of the Father, he hath declared him.

Matt. 3:17:

And lo a voice from heaven, saying, This is my beloved Son, in whom I am well pleased.

Read carefully Matt. 21:33-46.   See John 1:12, 13; also Gal. 3:26.

(3)   Christian Science denies the true doctrine of sin.

Christian Science says: "Belief in sin is an error; in reality, there is no evil; the soul cannot sin; sin is not real; sin is an illusion."   Through the denial of error [instead of through His stripes] we are healed. In the Lord's Prayer as used by them, the phrases "forgive us our debts," and "deliver us from evil" are explained away.   That this is contrary to the teaching of the Scriptures is evident from a study of the following references:

Rom. 5:12:

> Wherefore, as by one man sin entered into the world, and death by sin; and so death passed upon all men, for that all have sinned.

Ezek. 18:4:

> Behold, all souls are mine; as the soul of the father, so also the soul of the son is mine; the soul that sinneth, it shall die.

See also Jas. 1:15, and John 8:21-24.

The Scriptures clearly teach us that Jesus Christ came into the world to die for sin. If there be no such thing as sin in the world, then Jesus Christ died for a tremendous unreality.

8. "God is too good to condemn any one."

You may ask the question to what we are indebted for our conception of the character of God—is it not to the Bible? On what do we build our hope of the future—is it not on the Bible? What picture of God, therefore, does the Bible present? Here is the question the worker should ask. It is true that the Bible presents God as love (1 John 4:8); it also presents Him as "a consuming fire" (Heb. 12:29). In 2 Peter 3:9 God is set forth as both loving and just.

(a) Show the purpose of God's goodness and the danger of abusing it.

This may be done by the use of Romans 2:4, 5:

> Or despisest thou the riches of his goodness and forbearance and longsuffering; not knowing that the goodness of God leadeth thee to repentance?
> But after thy hardness and impenitent heart treasurest up unto thyself wrath against the day of wrath and revelation of the righteous judgment of God.

The context of this passage shows us that the Jews counted themselves within the pale of God's mercy,

while the Gentiles were regarded by them as outside of
this mercy, and that even though the Jews were incon-
sistent in life, they would be saved because they were
within the pale of God's mercy. The apostle shows
them that their reliance on God's tolerance to suspend
the rule of His administration in their case is virtual
contempt. They are thereby simply storing up to
themselves wrath because of their abuse of God's mercy.

Romans 2:4, 5:

> Or despisest thou the riches of His goodness and for-
> bearance and longsuffering; not knowing that the good-
> ness of God leadeth thee to repentance?
> But after thy hardness and impenitent heart treasurest
> up unto thyself wrath against the day of wrath and
> revelation of the righteous judgment of God.

Show them from these verses the purpose of God's
goodness—to lead them to repentance.

Ezek. 33:11 and 2 Peter 3:9-11 teach us, that, while
God longs to have us saved, yet if we do not turn from
our sins, judgment, though temporarily suspended, will
finally fall upon us.

*(b) It will be well to show the inquirer that the
revelation of God we possess in the Bible, distinctly declares that the goodness of God does not prohibit His
justice being executed.* For this purpose use

2 Peter 2:4-6:

> For if God spared not the angels that sinned, but
> cast them down to hell, and delivered them into chains
> of darkness, to be reserved unto judgment;
> And spared not the old world, but saved Noah the
> eighth person, a preacher of righteousness, bringing in
> the flood upon the world of the ungodly;
> And turning the cities of Sodom and Gomorrah into
> ashes, condemned them with an overthrow, making them
> an ensample unto those that after should live ungodly.

These verses not only show what God did do, but
also what God will do. Indeed, we are told that what
He did to the Antediluvians was an ensample to the
ungodly.

(c) Finally, read Matthew 25:31-46.

9. The Millennial Dawnist.

We here set forth a general view of the doctrines of this phase of religious belief, and some brief suggestions as to how to answer them.

1. Millennial Dawnism denies the deity and the humanity of Jesus Christ.

Its faith may be expressed somewhat in this manner:

Jesus Christ was not always divine; He was a created being of the very highest order; a god, but not God; He was called God only in an inferior and derived sense; He is never called Jehovah anywhere in the Scriptures, nor does He declare Himself to be God; like Adam, He was merely a man, untainted and sinless —but only a man, and consequently mortal. His death was the death of a mere man. His human nature had to be consecrated to death before He could receive even the pledge of the divine nature. Not until He had actually sacrificed the human nature even unto death did He become partaker of the divine nature, and since His resurrection He is what He never was before, that is, *a God.* Only in this sense do the Millennial Dawnists acknowledge Christ as divine.

Christ's humanity is denied. Jesus Christ is no longer a man. At the resurrection His body evaporated into gases, or is preserved by God as a memorial in some secluded part of the universe. The body of Jesus Christ was not raised at the resurrection. What was raised was an entirely new creation, and not the body which had been put in the tomb. When Christ died His entire humanity died with Him, and was not raised again.

How to Meet This False Belief.

(a) Show that the Scriptures assert the real deity of Christ.

John 1 :1 :

> In the beginning was the Word, and the Word was with God, and the Word was God.

This verse teaches that the Word was not from, but in the beginning; that the Word was God, not *a God*. If the objection is made that the "Word" here refers to spoken utterances and not to Jesus Christ, the 14th verse, clearly indicates that the "Word" in verse 1 is the incarnate Word.

Col. 1 :16, 17 :

> For by him were all things created, that are in heaven, and that are in earth, visible and invisible, whether they be thrones, or dominions, or principalities, or powers; all things were created by him, and for him:
> And he is before all things, and by him all things consist.

These verses show that Jesus Christ was not a created being, but the Creator of all existing beings. In other words, the Christ of Colossians 1 is the God of Genesis 1. Millennial Dawnism is a revival of Gnosticism with which Paul deals so fully in Colossians.

That the fulness of the Godhead dwelt bodily in Christ, both before and during His incarnation, is evidenced from Colossians 2 :9.

A comparison of John 8 :58 with Exodus 3 :13 shows that we may legitimately say that Christ applied the name Jehovah to Himself. In John 12 :38-41 it is distinctly stated that the glory of Jehovah which Israel saw was the glory of the Christ of the New Testament.

Further, a comparison of 1 Cor. 2 :11 with John 1 :18, shows clearly that no mere human being could reveal God.

(b) Show that the Scriptures assert the real humanity of Christ.

The Millennial Dawnist denies the humanity of Christ. In contradistinction to this belief, the Apostle

Paul clearly and distinctly affirms the humanity of Christ in 1 Tim. 2:5:

> For there is one God, and one mediator between God and men, the man Christ Jesus;

Christ himself asserts the reality of His resurrection body, and indeed its identity, with the body He had before His resurrection:

Luke 24:39:

> Behold my hands and my feet, that it is I myself: handle me, and see; for a spirit hath not flesh and bones, as ye see me have.

It was the Son of Man whom Stephen saw in his dying vision (Acts 7:56). It is the *same* Christ of whose identity the disciples were assured (Luke 24:39), and whose person Thomas was allowed to scrutinize and handle (John 20:24-29), whom the angels announced is coming again personally and visibly (Acts 1:11).

2. *Millennial Dawnism denies the true Scriptural teaching of the Holy Spirit.*

The following is taken from Mr. Russell's work, *The Atonement*, pages 165-166: "And equally consistent is the Scriptural teaching regarding the Holy Spirit, that it is not another God, but the spirit, influence, or power exercised by the one God, our Father. The Three-in-One doctrine suits well the dark ages."

(a) The Scripture clearly teaches both the personality and deity of the Holy Spirit.

In John 16:13, 14, the personal pronoun "he" is seven times used of the Holy Ghost. It is true that in Rom. 8:16 the neuter pronoun "itself" is used, but the Revised Version properly translates the word "himself."

Personal acts are ascribed to the Holy Spirit: He speaks; He searches the deep things of God; He makes intercession; He takes the place of a person, the Lord

Jesus Christ (Rev. 2:7; 1 Cor. 2:10; Rom. 8:26; John 14:16). He may be lied against and blasphemed (Acts 5:3; Matt. 12:31, 32).

If the Holy Spirit were not a divine person it would hardly seem right to use His name as being of equal importance and majesty with that of the Father and Son, as is done in the baptism formula (Matt. 28:19), and the Apostolic benediction (2 Cor. 13:14).

3. *Millennial Dawnism believes in probation after death.*

It declares that the impenitent will have a second opportunity to accept the Gospel. "The ransom for all, given by the man, Christ Jesus, does not guarantee or give everlasting life or blessing to every man, but it does guarantee to every man another trial for life everlasting. The restoration to perfect human nature will be accomplished gradually during the millennial age— 'the time of restitution.'"

The parable of the Rich Man and Lazarus (Luke 16:19-31) distinctly teaches us that the period of human probation ends at death, and that the state in which death finds a man is the state in which he shall remain during all eternity.

Compare also the following passages: Revelation 22:11, which teaches that as death and the judgment finds a man, so he will remain throughout all eternity; 2 Corinthians 6:2, which distinctly states that "Now is the day of salvation"; Hebrews 2:3, which shows us that there is no escape in the future for any rejection of the Gospel in this life; John 5:28, 29, clearly teach that the wicked are raised not for the purpose of being given a second chance, but for the purpose of receiving their judgment of condemnation.

THE OBSTINATE

CHAPTER XIV.

X. THE OBSTINATE.

THERE are some people who, like Pharaoh of old, sin against God with a high hand and a hard face. They say: "Who is the Lord, that I should serve and obey Him? Away with you, I don't want to hear about God and your religion." They have made up their minds firmly to pursue an evil course. Like Ahab of old, they have determined not to serve God, and, seemingly, no quality of human effort on the part of the most earnest Christian has the slightest influence in turning them from their evil course.

This class of people may be recognized by the following excuses:

1. "I don't want you to talk to me."

The duty of the Christian worker is to talk to them anyway. We must not shirk our duty of speaking to and warning them against the error of their ways. The following passages are helpful in dealing with this class:

Jer. 1:17:

> Thou therefore gird up thy loins, and arise, and speak unto them all that I command thee: be not dismayed at their faces, lest I confound thee before them.

Ezek. 3:11:

> And go, get thee to them of the captivity, unto the children of thy people, and speak unto them, and tell them, Thus saith the Lord God; whether they will hear, or whether they will forbear.

2 Cor. 2:15-17:

> For we are unto God a sweet savour of Christ, in them that are saved, and in them that perish:

To the one we are the savour of death unto death, and to the other the savour of life unto life. And who is sufficient for these things?

For we are not as many, which corrupt the word of God: but as of sincerity, but as of God, in the sight of God speak we in Christ.

Show them the punishment for such stout obstinacy; that such imperiousness cannot escape judgment.

Psa. 81:12:

So I gave them up unto their own hearts' lust: and they walked in their own counsels.

Eccl. 11:9; Rom. 2:8, 9.

Rom. 1:21-25:

Because that, when they knew God, they glorified him not as God, neither were thankful; but became vain in their imaginations, and their foolish heart was darkened.

Professing themselves to be wise, they became fools,

And changed the glory of the uncorruptible God into an image made like to corruptible man, and to birds, and fourfooted beasts, and creeping things.

Wherefore God also gave them up to uncleanliness, through the lusts of their own hearts, to dishonor their own bodies between themselves:

Who changed the truth of God into a lie, and worshipped and served the creature more than the Creator, who is blessed for ever. Amen.

Rev. 22:11:

He that is unjust, let him be unjust still: and he which is filthy, let him be filthy still: and he that is righteous, let him be righteous still: and he that is holy, let him be holy still.

2. "I want to have my own way."

Well, that is their prerogative; but show them what God thinks about this unreasonable desire:

Prov. 14:12:

There is a way which seemeth right unto a man; but the end thereof are the ways of death.

Prov. 12:15:

The way of a fool is right in his own eyes: but he that hearkeneth unto counsel is wise.

Prov. 30:12:

> There is a generation that are pure in their own eyes, and yet is not washed from their filthiness.

Matt. 7:13, 14:

> Enter ye in at the strait gate: for wide is the gate, and broad is the way, that leadeth to destruction, and many, there be which go in thereat:
> Because strait is the gate, and narrow is the way, which leadeth unto life, and few there be that find it.

1 Pet. 4:17, 18:

> For the time is come that judgment must begin at the house of God: and if it first begin at us, what shall the end be of them that obey not the gospel of God?
> And if the righteous scarcely be saved, where shall the ungodly and the sinner appear?

3. "I have made up my mind to have a good time in this world, and I don't care about the world to come."

(a) Show the folly of this course:

Luke 16:25:

> But Abraham said, Son, remember that thou in thy lifetime receivedst thy good things, and likewise Lazarus evil things: but now he is comforted, and thou art tormented.

Luke 12:15:

> And he said unto them, Take heed, and beware of covetousness: for a man's life consisteth not in the abundance of the things which he possesseth.

Luke 12:19-21:

> And I will say to my soul, Soul, thou hast much goods laid up for many years; take thine ease, eat, drink, and be merry.
> But God said unto him, Thou fool, this night thy soul shall be required of thee: then whose shall those things be, which thou hast provided?
> So is he that layeth up treasure for himself, and is not rich toward God.

1 Cor. 15:32, 34:

> If after the manner of men I have fought with beasts at Ephesus, what advantageth it me, if the dead rise not? let us eat and drink; for tomorrow we die.
> Awake to righteousness, and sin not; for some have not the knowledge of God: I speak this to your shame.

(b) Show that God will judge them for these things:

Eccl. 11:9:

> Rejoice, O young man, in thy youth; and let thy heart cheer thee in the days of thy youth, and walk in the ways of thine heart, and in the sight of thine eyes: but know thou, that for all these things God will bring thee into judgment.

2 Pet. 2:12:

> But these, as natural brute beasts made to be taken and destroyed, speak evil of the things that they understand not; and shall utterly perish in their own corruption.

See also Rom. 2:5-11.

THE SKEPTIC

CHAPTER XV.

XI. THE SKEPTIC.

THE Christian worker who is anxious for the promulgation of God's kingdom on earth, must equip himself to meet those forms of unbelief so prevalent in our day. Mere arguments, elaborately stated and eloquently discussed, cannot meet this great need of turning the night of infidelity into the day of Christian light. The Word of God alone, as used by the Holy Spirit, can turn our darkness into light, and our unbelief into faith. Our arguments should not be "carnal" but "spiritual."

There are two classes of skeptics—the insincere, and the serious-minded. In dealing with them, it is well to find out by asking questions to which class they belong.

THE INSINCERE SKEPTIC.

In dealing with the insincere skeptic, you may use the following method:

(a) Show the cause of his skepticism.
This may be done by the use of:

Rom. 1:25, 28:

> Who changed the truth of God into a lie, and worshipped and served the creature more than the Creator, who is blessed forever.
> And even as they did not like to retain God in their knowledge, God gave them over to a reprobate mind, to do those things which are not convenient.

These verses reveal the real cause of skepticism. At its root, its cause is moral rather than intellectual. It would be well to read verses 19-28 entire to the inquirer. Seek to find out if there is not some sin in his life that is the cause of his skepticism.

Also John 8:47:

> He that is of God heareth God's words: ye therefore hear them not, because ye are not of God.

(b) Show the fatal consequences of such skepticism.

2 Thess. 2:10, 12:

> And with all deceivableness of unrighteousness in them that perish; because they received not the love of the truth, that they might be saved.
> That they all might be damned who believed not the truth, but had pleasure in unrighteousness.

Also 2 Thess. 1:7-9.

THE EARNEST-MINDED SKEPTIC.

Some skeptics claim to be sincere in their skepticism. They profess to desire to believe, but find themselves unable to do so. This class of skeptics may express themselves in the following way:

"I cannot believe."

Ask them just what they think "believing" is. Show them that the faith which they are called upon to exercise in order to be saved is of the same nature as that which they are called upon to use, and indeed, are using, daily in business, social and domestic life—the only difference being in the object of that faith. To believe in a person is to accept what that person says about himself or anything else, as being true, and to relate oneself to him as one who thus believes in him. The man in business makes an engagement with you to meet you at a certain time and place. The fact that you meet him at that appointed time and place is an evidence of your belief in him and his word. That is faith in everyday life. Now transfer that to the higher —the spiritual realm. God says certain things concerning His relation to men and their salvation. For example, God says that all men have sinned (1 John 1:8-10), and are, therefore, under wrath and condemnation (John 3:18, 19, 36); but that He so loved us, sinful though we were and are, that He gave his Son to die for us (Rom. 5:6-8), in order that the wrath and penalty due to our sin might fall on Christ, our sinless substitute, and not on us (Gal. 3:13; 2 Cor. 5:21; 1 Peter 2:24); and, therefore, if any man will believe God's testimony concerning these things (1 John 5:9-12), he has everlasting life and shall not come into condemnation (John 5:24). If we receive the witness of men (1 John 5:9, 10)—and we do, daily—why should we not receive the witness of God?

(a) The way to find out whether or not a thing is true and worthy of one's acceptance is to put this thing to the test. So we are told in

John 7:17; Hosea 6:3.

If any man will do his will, he shall know of the doctrine, whether it be of God, or whether I speak of myself.

Notice how this verse reads, especially in the Revised Version. We get to know the truth of what God says by obedience to that truth. Ordinarily we seek to find out whether a thing is true or not before we do it, and if we are persuaded that it is true, we then do it. But God's ways are not our ways. God tells us to obey the doctrine, to do His will, and in the doing of it we shall discover the truth of it. We do first, then we know.

It is well, therefore, to ask the inquirer if he will do the things God asks him to do. For example, we are told in the Bible that "God is, and that He is a rewarder of them that diligently seek Him" (Heb. 11:6); that He is a prayer-hearing and prayer-answering God, one who is nigh unto all those that call upon Him in truth (Psa. 145:18); that He gives assurance, peace and joy to those that keep His commandments (Isa. 32:17; John 14:27; John 1:4). Now, the question for the inquirer to settle is, whether or not he will live his life as in the presence of God, call upon Him fervently and sincerely in prayer, and lead a life that is lived in obedience to God's known commands. If so, this shows that he is a sincere seeker after truth, for he is willing to follow all the light that he can get. If he is not willing to do this, he does not deserve to be classed among the earnest-minded skeptics.

(b) It will be well to show him the conditions of salvation as laid down in the Bible.

This may be done by referring to pages 65-70.

SOME SKEPTICAL OBJECTIONS.

1. "I don't believe in the existence of God."

The Bible does not undertake to prove the existence of God. It asserts it; it takes it for granted. The sacred volume introduces itself to us with the sublime words, "In the beginning God created the heaven and the earth." (Gen. 1:1.) This sublime statement at once contradicts Pantheism, which believes that God is the universe, and the universe is God. It contradicts the unity of matter, and asserts the independency of God over matter and His separateness from it.

But while the Bible nowhere undertakes to prove the existence of God—always, and everywhere taking it for granted—yet it leaves us not without indications and evidences of the fact that there is, and always has been, and ever will be, a living, intelligent, personal Being whom we adore and worship as God.

"In a musical instrument, when we observe divers stops meet in harmony, we conclude that some skillful musician tuned them. When we see thousands of men in a field, marshaled under several colors, all yielding exact obedience, we infer that there is a general, whose command they are all subject to. In a watch, when we take notice of great and small wheels, all so fitted as to concur in an orderly motion, we acknowledge the skill of an artificer. When we come into a printing office, and see a great number of different letters so ordered as to make a book, it is evident that there is a composer, by whose art they have been brought into such a frame. When we behold a fair building, we conclude it had an architect; a stately ship, well-rigged, and safely conducted to the port, that it hath a pilot. So here the visible world is such an instrument, army, watch, book, building, ship, as undeniably argueth a God, who was and is the tuner, general, and artificer, the composer, architect, and pilot of it."

With the above thought in view, see

Rom. 1:19, 22:

> Because that which may be known of God is manifest in them; for God hath shewed it unto them.
> For the invisible things of him from the creation of the world are clearly seen, being understood by the things that are made, even his eternal power and Godhead; so that they are without excuse.

Psalm 8:1, 3:

> O Lord our Lord, how excellent is thy name in all the earth! who hast set thy glory above the heavens.
> When I consider thy heavens, the work of thy fingers, the moon and the stars, which thou hast ordained.

Psalm 33:6:

> By the word of the Lord were the heavens made; and all the host of them by the breath of his mouth.

No man can be counted really wise (Psa. 14:1) who, in the face of such evidences as these, doubts the existence of an all-wise, all-ruling, personal God.

2. "I don't believe in future eternal punishment."

The argument commonly used against future punishment is the incompatibility of God's love with such a doctrine. We must not let our sympathy run away with our judgment, however. We must not forget that, while the Bible asserts that God is "love," it also tells us that God is "just." We have no more authority for believing the one than the other. Both statements are equally clear and emphatic. Love is not an effeminate tenderness—a weak, womanish sympathy, that cannot punish the disobedient. There was a time when the terror of the law was preached too much; now the pendulum has swung over to the other extreme—too much love.

The question: Is there a hell? resolves itself into this: Is there a moral Governor of the world? Is there a moral law? Is there such a thing as sin? For, if there be, then there is such a thing as punishment for sin. There is sin, and there is punishment for sin which we daily witness. But there is not for all sin such a reckoning in this world as meets the claims of righteousness and justice. Do we not daily see evil doings pass undetected, and many bad men pass unpunished? See how often the righteous suffer and the wicked flourish. When we take a deliberate view of these things we are led to exclaim, "Wherefore do the wicked live, become old, yea, are mighty in power?" Is there no reward for the righteous? Is there no punishment for the workers of iniquity? Is there no God that judgeth in the earth? And, indeed, were there no retribution beyond the limits of the present life, we should be necessarily obliged to admit one or the other of the following conclusions: Either that no moral Governor of the world exists, or that justice and judgment are not the habitation of His throne.

See the following passages:

Luke 16:23-26:

And in hell he lifted up his eyes, being in torments, and seeth Abraham afar off, and Lazarus in his bosom.

And he cried and said, Father Abraham, have mercy on me, and send Lazarus, that he may dip the tip of his finger in water, and cool my tongue; for I am tormented in this flame.

But Abraham said, Son, remember that thou in thy lifetime receivedst thy good things, and likewise Lazarus evil things: but now he is comforted, and thou art tormented.

And beside all this, between us and you there is a great gulf fixed: so that they which would pass from hence to you cannot; neither can they pass to us, that would come from thence.

Luke 12:5:

But I will forewarn you whom ye shall fear: Fear him, which after he hath killed hath power to cast into hell; yea, I say unto you, Fear him.

Matt. 25:41, 46:

Then shall he say also unto them on the left hand, Depart from me, ye cursed, into everlasting fire, prepared for the devil and his angels:

And these shall go away into everlasting punishment: but the righteous into life eternal.

Mark 9:43, 44:

And if thy hand offend thee, cut it off: it is better for thee to enter into life maimed, than having two hands to go into hell, into the fire that never shall be quenched:

Where their worm dieth not, and the fire is not quenched.

3. "I don't believe in the inspiration of the Bible."

Let us not fear that the unbelief of men in this sacred volume will ultimately cause its overthrow. Heaven and earth may pass away, but one jot or tittle of God's Word shall never pass away till all be fulfilled. (Matt. 5:18.)

Let us show them:

(a) That their unbelief does not make God's Word void.

Rom. 3:3, 4:

For what if some did not believe? shall their unbelief make the faith of God without effect?

God forbid: yea, let God be true, but every man a liar; as it is written, That thou mightest be justified in thy sayings, and mightest overcome when thou art judged.

(b) The testimony of the Scriptures to their inspiration.

2 Tim. 3:16:

All scripture is given by inspiration of God, and is profitable for doctrine, for reproof, for correction, for instruction in righteousness:

See, also, 2 Peter 2:19-21; 1 Thess. 2:13; 2 Sam. 23:2; Heb. 4:12; Jer. 23:27, 28.

Compare also Psalm 119, and see how often David calls the Scriptures God's "Word," "law," "statute," "testimonies," etc.

4. "I do not believe in the deity of Christ."

See under "The Unitarian," page 142.